Reflections on
The Architecture
of
Williams College

Reflections on The Architecture of Williams College

Whitney S. Stoddard *Author*

Thomas W. Bleezarde *Editor*

Arthur D. Evans *Photographer*

Foreword by William E. Simon Jr.
Preface by David C. Johnson

This publication contains more than 150 color illustrations taken by Arthur D. Evans. The work of
others has been indicated on the appropriate pic-
tures according to the following list of abbreviations:

Henry W. Art   HWA
Thomas W. Bleezarde   TWB
David Brown   DB
Cosmo Catalano   CC
A. Blake Gardner   ABG
John M. Kuykendahl   JMK
Cynthia Locklin   CL
Sylvia Salmi   SS
Irwin Shainman   IS
Whitney S. Stoddard   WSS
William H. Tague   WHT
Winthrop M. Wassenar   WMW
Nicholas Whitman   NW
Williams College Archives   WCA
Williams College Museum of Art   WCMA

The Tefft drawings of Lawrence Hall on page 39
were obtained from the Brown University Library
Archives. The Bowen woodcut on page 19, the
Trumbull drawing on page 22, and the Doolittle
photograph on page 23 are from the Manuscripts
and Archives department of the Yale University
Library.

ISBN 0-915081-05-9

Williams College
Williamstown, Massachusetts 01267

Book Design by Abigail Sturges Design
New York, New York

Printed in the United States of America by
Wolf ColorPrint, Newington, Connecticut 06111

(Pierson, 1954)

(WHT, 1970)

(Hirsche, 1987)

Dedication

H. Lee Hirsche (1927-1998)

This book is dedicated to H. Lee Hirsche, the creator of the Studio Art program at Williams. A member of the faculty from 1956 until 1984, he was an inspirational teacher, very much "into" all of the arts, including architecture.

Despite Lee's having to work in a series of makeshift quarters, his enthusiasm was contagious and his classes attracted steadily increasing numbers of students. He had a profound influence on a great many graduates who became architects, and he changed the lives of many students who became painters or sculptors. Because of the results of Lee's efforts, Studio Art became a major, taking its place in the Art Department along side Art History.

He made the "art of creating" an exciting experience, and through such devices as Kite Days and Rube Goldberg-esque sculpture shows, brought the work of his students to the attention of the campus and the Williamstown community.

Besides being a dynamic and demanding teacher, Lee was an accomplished painter, printmaker and sculptor. Examples of his work can be seen on the campus: the gilded cross in the choir of the Thompson Memorial Chapel; the sculptures in the open courtyard between Chapin Hall and the Bernhard Music Center.

Contents

Acknowledgments

The idea for this book grew from conversations between College Trustee William E. Simon Jr. '73 and David C. Johnson '71, Williams tennis and squash coach. Bill was a history major and took my Art 101 course in his sophomore year. Dave, another Art 101 veteran, was an art major and has an MA from the Williams/Clark Program in the History of Art. They discussed a picture book with text about the architecture of the college buildings and decided to move ahead with what they felt was a worthwhile idea.

I was approached to write the book since I had been lecturing to the freshmen classes for more than three decades about campus architecture and had made presentations to regional alumni associations on the same topic. I agreed to write it if I had editorial freedom to be critical when I thought it was warranted.

Vivian Patterson '77, curator of collections at the College Museum of Art, suggested I ask Tom Bleezarde, retiring as editor of the Williams Alumni Review, to serve as editor. I thought this was a wonderful idea and the collaboration between the two of us started and has been a lot of fun and I hope fruitful.

Many organizations and people have helped assemble the information on College buildings whether it be the Weston Field facility or the Thompson Memorial Chapel, to point out two extremes of size and beauty.

Major help came from Sylvia Kennick Brown, College archivist, and her able assistant, Linda Hall. Their photographic and historical files were an invaluable resource and their ability to quickly respond to requests for specific and sometimes obscure information was uncanny.

Sylvia and Linda also prepared the Bibliography and the Gone But Not Forgotten appendix, and read through the original draft of the text on a fact-checking mission. Other copy reading by former faculty members Fred Rudolph '42 and John M. Hyde '52 and current Associate Professor of Art Michael Lewis was most helpful.

During the early research stages, efficient and able help was provided by Robin Schuldenfrei, then a second-year student in the graduate program in art history.

Art Evans, a freelance photographer who has worked for WCMA, the Clark and MassMOCA, was selected to handle the vital photographic aspect of the book. He worked for a year and a half through a variety of weather and seasons, to produce color transparencies that have been used here.

Help was obtained from various people in Buildings and Grounds, especially from Director Win Wassenar and college architect Chris Williams, in the mapping of the tunnel system, and with information on the more recent buildings.

Viv Patterson has been a stalwart supporter throughout and has helped us find much-appreciated illustrations from the museum files. Former art professor William Pierson provided helpful guidance and consultation.

Faculty secretaries Peggy Weyers and Donna Chenail transcribed innumerable tapes and John LeClaire, proprietor of LeClaire Custom Color labs, provided essential darkroom skills.

Valuable contributions were also made by: Henry W. Art, professor of biology; Rhett Austell '44, John Shaw '61, Robert D. Kavanaugh, professor of psychology; Henry J. Bruton, emeritus professor of economics; Benjamin W. Labaree, emeritus professor of history; and Judy Reichert, wife of the former head of the Williams in Oxford program John F. Reichert. Their work is attributed in various portions of the book.

Dave Johnson and Bill Simon have remained intensely involved throughout the creative and production processes. Without their interest and support this volume would never have been published.

Whitney S. Stoddard
Williamstown, Massachusetts
September 2001

Foreword

What a great thrill and privilege to collaborate with Whit Stoddard and Dave Johnson on this architectural history of our beloved *alma mater*.

Whit, of course, is a seemingly eternal font of knowledge of Williams history, architectural and otherwise. Having graduated with the class of 1935 and taught art history for more than 44 years would certainly seem to be sufficient credentials, but as important, Whit's family includes a father who graduated in 1900, an uncle in 1908, a brother in 1932, and more recently a son, a daughter, a grandson and a granddaughter. Talk about a Williams family. Whit remembers attending reunion weekends as early as 1925 and he hasn't missed many since.

This work grew out of a desire to create a permanent record of Whit's recollections and opinions regarding all Williams matters architectural. These indelible recollections and strong opinions had been apparent for years to Whit's art history students, including Dave and me. Beginning in the early 1970s, his wisdom was revealed to a wider audience when he began a series of "Freshman Days" talks entitled *A Sense of Where You Are*, a building-by-building discussion full of historical notes, architectural insights and captivating anecdotes.

Whit and his subject were so popular that by the mid-1980s a second "rendition" was initiated. *A Sense of Where You Were* was presented during pre-Commencement "Senior Days," drawing audiences which included both those who remembered the earlier version and many of their classmates, drawn by the enthusiasm of their friends.

These lectures continued into the late 1990s, well after Whit had officially retired from the faculty, and were heard by thousands of Williams men and women, myself included. As alumni our fondness for Whit and for the Williams campus became instrumental in bringing Whit and his "architectural tour" to Regional Alumni Association meetings in all corners of the land.

Reflecting on my own Williams experience often reminds me of the important roles played by Whit and of the campus with which he is so familiar. I soon concluded that I should do what I could to preserve Whit's "tour" in a permanent form that could be readily referenced by those who had heard him in person, and to broaden his "audience," so that those who had missed his talk could at least read what he had to say.

My inclinations have delightfully evolved with the more than able assistance of Dave Johnson, whose Class of 1971 voted him the outstanding scholar athlete. For the past 12 years, Dave has been coach of squash and tennis at Williams. Dave has also earned his masters in art history in the Williams Graduate Program in Art History and has written on the history of a number of buildings, notably the Racquet and Tennis Club in New York. After three years of part time work in the Dean's office, he will join the Art 101 faculty this fall teaching three conference sections in the Introduction to the History of Art.

It was Dave's strong desire, with the quick concurrence of Whit and me, to expand our project to produce a work that all generations of the extended Williams family could reference as a comprehensive treatment of the archi-

tecture of the College buildings up to the date of publication.

Consistent with this expanded objective, we have attempted to consult all available sources of information. The scope of this work is intended to include all buildings constructed on the campus between 1790 and today.

As the reader might suspect, the history of Williams architecture is not without controversy, and we have not shied away from noting, or even expressing opinions about, buildings which may not epitomize a particular architectural style. These comments, it should be emphasized, came from a loving set of hands with the motivation to be as thorough and analytical as possible.

Throughout the text are tidbits of information about the layout of the campus; the history of various buildings (past, present and intended uses); diverse matters which raised controversy; and, where relevant, relationships between the College and the town.

Appendices discuss significant buildings which once served the College but no longer exist; former fraternity properties now owned by the College and their current functions; and College monuments which have become campus landmarks in their own right.

It is the hope of all of us who labored to bring this project to fruition that readers will find it enjoyable, informative and inspirational. We wish you good reading!

William E. Simon Jr.
Los Angeles, California
October 2001

9

Preface

I remember my first impression of Whitney Stoddard from nearly thirty-five years ago as if it were yesterday.

I had signed up for Art 101 on the advice of a close family friend and Williams alumnus. He had suggested that whatever preconceived ideas about art history I might have would be quickly changed if I took this course. Although sure he was just spinning me a line to get me to diversify my academic interests, I took his advice.

I arrived for my first class on a hot and humid September morning in the cavernous upstairs lecture room in Lawrence Hall and quickly took a seat in the very back. My assumption was that the lectures would be very boring and staking out a territorial claim to a secluded seating area where a quick nap in future classes would go unnoticed by the professor was an important course-survival strategy.

In through the main door at the rear of the auditorium came a nattily dressed man - seersucker jacket, dress shirt and bow tie. He strode energetically down the aisle to my right and up to the lectern at the front of the room. Looking up from the podium with a tilt of his head, so he could survey the class over the top of his reading glasses, he introduced himself as Professor Whitney Stoddard. "Gentlemen, welcome to Art 101," he intoned in a formal professorial baritone.

Then, stepping away from the lectern, Professor Stoddard begged the forgiveness of the class, asking rhetorically if anyone would mind if, due to the heat in the room, he took off his jacket. Not needing a reply, he carefully draped his coat over a nearby chair, and then readied his notes for the first slide.

But, to my astonishment, standing before me now was the same 'distinguished' professor with arms bare from the top of the shoulders on down. His Brooks Brothers oxford had been surgically de-sleeved at the very top of each shoulder, making it appear as if it had been designed as a sleeveless cutoff! Needless to say, Whit had claimed my full attention, and judging by the chorus of amused chuckles from those around me, other nonbelievers had been immediately converted as well.

To this day, this sketch still captures the Whit Stoddard I know. Hopefully, many of you reading this book will remember this same personality from your days at Williams. He has been a man whose great intelligence, tremendous range of intellectual interests and, above all, whose deep love for art and architecture has been constant, as has his mildly irreverent and totally unique sense of humor. His personality, intellect and presence are as powerful as any other that I have encountered in my nearly twenty years here at Williams College.

I can honestly say that Whit Stoddard is the single most important reason that I ended up enjoying my four years at Williams, I became an Art History major along the way and then, thanks to the power of Whit's recommendation, went on to architecture school at UPenn.

When I returned to Williams in the fall of 1989, my career in architecture somehow displaced by one in squash and tennis, Whit was the first person I sought out. With his encouragement, I returned to the field that he had introduced me to and which I had sorely missed, earning my Masters degree through the Graduate Program in Art History at the Clark Art Institute. More importantly, I returned to Whit's classroom as well, attending as many of his lectures as possible.

I rarely missed his welcome to first-year students, *A Sense of Where You Are*, or his good-bye to the seniors, *A Sense of Where You Were*. Laughter filled the auditorium, just as it always did when Whit spoke, and his dialogue on the campus, its buildings and its history, never failed to be as fresh, insightful and entertaining as if it were the first time he had spoken on the subject.

The more I listened, the more I realized just how precious and irreplaceable was Whit's knowledge about, and perspective on, the campus and its architecture. I began bothering him on a regular basis about getting to work on a book that would be, in effect, a walking tour of the campus. Whit's gift in lecturing was in making his listeners feel that they were sharing in a private, informal dialogue where the occasional, humorous family secret would be revealed with no holds barred. It is this conversational quality of Whit's speaking which I hope this book has captured.

While it is not the intent of this book to be the definitive history of the college and its buildings, Whit's recollections and his historical perspective on the changing campus life, particularly with regard to the various personalities he has encountered in more than sixty years of Williams associations, are of inestimable value to the heritage of this institution. The personality and dry sense of humor that have been unique to Whit's lecturing style are captured by the "Whiticisms" that appear on many of the pages.

With advice and consul from my friend and colleague, EJ Johnson, Class of 1955 Professor of Art History and heir to the Stoddard legacy as the benevolent godfather of Art 101, a team was put in place to help Whit move his words from lecture to written and pictorial format. EJ's incredible respect for, and deep friendship with Whit have positively affected the course of this project from day one.

Robin Schuldenfrei, then a graduate student in the Clark Program and now on to a doctoral program at Harvard, was the first to organize the effort, which involved the sleuthing skills of Sylvia Kennick Brown, college archivist and Williamsiana curator, as well as the administrative talents of Donna Chenail, coordinator of the Faculty Secretarial Office.

Art Evans, whose astounding photographs you will see herein, has painstakingly waited for the right combination of conditions over four seasons of Williamstown weather to trip his shutter and freeze forever a Williams building or detail at just the right instant. Many times, when he was not satisfied with his initial result,

he returned to shoot again. His painstaking work has produced unforgettable images.

Tom Bleezarde, former editor of the *Williams Alumni Review*, rode to the rescue of a project in need of continued stewardship and brought the book through all of its various editing stages, then to an art director and publisher and finally into your hands as the beautifully detailed and executed book that it is. Tom originally promised just a month of his time to do a quick edit of the manuscript, but has now devoted more than a year and a half of his energy and professional expertise to Whit and his book.

However, there is one person (other than Whit!) whose love and care for this endeavor has truly allowed it all to happen as I envisioned. When I first shared my ideas about Whit and this book with my very dear friend and former Williams squash and tennis teammate, Bill Simon, he immediately fell in love with the project. At that moment, the reality of bringing it to completion was finally viable.

Bill, Williams '73 and now a Trustee of the College, has been active on a number of the college's major initiatives and will no doubt figure prominently in many more in the years to come, but his generosity, constant encouragement and vision have clearly been the backbone of this undertaking. Without his unqualified support, this book would still be in the concept stage; it would certainly never ever have gone to press. I hope he is as pleased as I am with our efforts. At first, it wasn't easy to get Whit to sit down to this project – he was

always too busy! Once underway, however, Whit threw himself into this undertaking with all of the energy and enthusiasm of a first-year graduate student. He has personally supervised the design of each and every page, from the selection of photographs to the editing of each word of the text.

In fact, this book is as much a reflection of Whitney Stoddard as it is of the architecture of Williams College. This fall, on the grand occasion of Whit's receiving an honorary degree from his beloved *alma mater*, I can think of no greater celebration of his dedication and devotion to this institution than the release of this book.

Whitney, on behalf of a half century of Williams students who sat in your classrooms and learned to love art and architecture because of who you are and what you told us, I hope this book will serve, at the very least, as a small "thank you" for your life's work here at Williams College.

David C. Johnson
Williamstown, Massachusetts
October 6, 2001

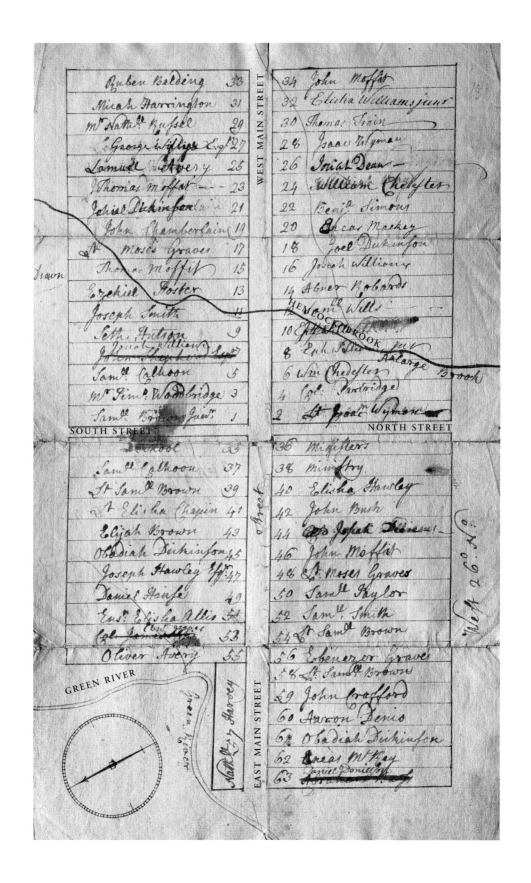

WEST MAIN STREET (center vertical label)

Ruben Belding 33	34 John Moffat
Micah Harrington 31	32 Elisha Williams junr
Mr Nathl Russel 29	30 Thomas Train
George Wyllys Esqr 27	28 Isaac Wyman
Samuel Avery 25	26 Josiah Dean
Thomas Moffat 23	24 William Chidester
Jehiel Dickinson 21	22 Benjn Simons
John Chamberlain 19	20 Lucas Mackey
Moses Graves 17	18 Joel Dickinson
Thomas Moffit 15	16 Josiah Williams
Ezekiel Foster 13	14 Abner Robards
Joseph Smith 11	Henry Wells
Seth Hutson 9	10
John Shepherd Esq	8 Erick
Saml Calhoon 5	6 Wm Chidester
Mr Timo Woodbridge 3	4 Col Partridge
Saml Brown junr 1	2 Lt Isaac Wyman

HEMLOCK BROOK (curved label across)

Alarge Brook

Seawn

SOUTH STREET —— **NORTH STREET**

School 35	36 Ministers
Saml Calhoon 37	38 Ministry
Lt Saml Brown 39	40 Elisha Hawley
Lt Elisha Chapin 41	42 John Bush
Elijah Brown 43	44 Josiah Stevens
Obadiah Dickinson 45	46 John Moffat
Joseph Hawley Esqr 47	48 Lt Moses Graves
Daniel Hawse 49	50 Saml Taylor
Ens Elisha Allis 51	52 Samll Smith
Col 53	54 Lt Saml Brown
Oliver Avery 55	56 Ebenezer Graves
	58 Lt Saml Brown
	59 John Crafford
	60 Aaron Denio
	61 Obadiah Dickinson
	62 Lucas McKey
	63

Street (vertical label)

GREEN RIVER

Green River

Math No 7 Hadley

EAST MAIN STREET (vertical label)

W.M 26 No

Introduction

The chartering of Williams College in 1793 was an act of faith and certainly an act surpassing the modest intentions of Colonel Ephraim Williams, for whom the college is named.

Williams was born in 1715 in Newton, Mass., into a gentry family whose positions in the military, church and judiciary ensured the support of family interests in the Bay Colony. In 1737, after schooling and three years of traveling throughout the world, Williams moved with his father's family to four townships in the Berkshires that his father had purchased from the resident Indian tribe. He worked for a time as a surveyor and manager of family interests, then was commissioned a captain and assigned command of a line of forts along the northern border of Massachusetts.

He made his headquarters in Fort Massachusetts, situated by the Hoosic River between the future towns of North Adams and Williamstown and was often in Stockbridge and Boston, tending to "military, family and personal business."

A survey was conducted in 1749, according to a plan drawn by Col. Williams, creating a town that he wanted to establish as a place for his soldiers to settle their families and educate their children.

The survey was carried out by Col. Nathaniel Dwight, and in 1750 Col. Miller and Capt. Lawrence laid out house lots. Their project was made more difficult then it might have been by the thickly wooded nature of the three-eighths of a mile wide area between the Green River and the Hemlock Brook in which they worked.

The survey defined 63 lots that were put on sale in 1751. They sold quite rapidly to the soldiers. Eph, himself, bought two (lots 8 and 10) on the north side of the street, straddling Hemlock Brook. The survey map shows a 250-foot-wide right-of-way, running west to east down the middle, where our East and West Main Streets are today. Hemlock Brook cuts through the upper center and the Green River is at the bottom.

The lots were ample, more than 80-feet wide and very, very long to accommodate animals and gardens. Indeed, additional land across the Hoosic River on the slopes of what is now Pine Cobble went with each lot for gardening and pastures.

Eph's plan centered on Hemlock Brook, but as the town developed most of the activity was to the east of the original survey area, along the banks of the Green River.

Williams had not intended to found a college. En route with his regiment of Massachusetts militia to join the battle with the French and Indians at Lake George, the Colonel had tarried long enough in Albany to write his last will and testament, on July 22, 1755. In it he bequeathed his residuary estate for the founding and support of a free school in West Township (Williamstown).

The will stipulated that West Township, then in dispute between Massachusetts and New York, must fall within Massachusetts and that the name of the township must be changed to Williamstown, if the free school was to be established at all. On September 8, 1755, Col. Williams was killed at the Battle of Lake George. On October 26, 1791, after many delays, 15 scholars were admitted to the free school in Williamstown.

Within a year the trustees, not content with the original modest design of the founder, were captivated by the idea of creating a college where, as they put it, "young gentlemen from every part of the Union" might resort for instruction "in all the branches of useful and polite literature."

On June 22, 1793, the Commonwealth of Massachusetts granted a charter to Williams College. Williams became the twenty-first institution of higher learning in the onetime British colonies, the second in Massachusetts, and the sixth in New England.

N.B. Throughout this book magnetic compass directions are used to define spatial relationships and viewpoints of the photographer and the reader, following the pattern used by Eph Williams in his plan of the town.

Part One

Early Buildings
1790–1842

*Hopkins Observatory,
from the north, original
location (WCA)*

West College

1793

West College, constructed between 1791 and 1793 to contain the entire College, appears at first glance to be quite a simple structure. It is really very subtle and has a great deal of architectural quality.

More than in any other building on the campus, West's deceptively simple design reveals, on close scrutiny, numerous subtleties. For instance, the windows on each side are in two vertical columns on the ends with five columns in the middle. This is a very subtle design distinction, one that has absolutely nothing to do with what goes on inside the building. The string courses, bricks standing on edge, change position from floor to floor. They are centered between the windows on the first and second floors, are subtly higher between the second and third floors, and are finally quite high just underneath the fourth floor windows.

The Trustees had directed that the school should be built on the town's two eminences and stipulated that the first building should be built on the western hill, on the highest ground in Williamstown. Building on the hills was an attempt to take advantage of the views and to make the structures a kind of monument.

No source of water was found near the site, so students used a spring at the foot of what is now Spring Street. Of course, in those days the building had no running water. Outhouses were constructed nearby, probably on what is now the lab campus.

West was positioned so that it was necessary to run the town sidewalk,

From the east

"Appears simple, but really very subtle"

an east/west footpath, through a hall in the middle of the building. The south half of the first floor held the dining room and the kitchen. On the second and third floors, south of a central hallway, was a two-story chapel with a balcony for the President and his entourage. These areas were probably also used as classrooms. The north end of the ground floor contained the President's office and living quarters. Above that, on the third floor, there was a room for the library which has been described as small enough that a librarian, standing in the middle of the room, could reach every book. The north end of the third floor and the entire fourth floor housed students in an open dormitory. A separate room on the fourth floor was designated for the bellringers and there was also a proctor nearby.

The doorway now on the east side is relatively new and has no relationship to Williamstown in the 1790s. It was designed in 1952 by the firm of Perry, Shaw and Hepburn, famous for their work at Williamsburg for the Rockefellers. However, Williamstown is not Williamsburg, and this doorway, installed after the 1951 fire, has absolutely no connection with what was being done architecturally in 1791–92.

The College, tired of having the town sidewalk running through the building, had earlier blocked off the east and the west entrances and created north and south doorways. Then, in the very early 20th century, the north entrance was closed and an east door was reinstalled. Despite all of these changes, the building's wonderful, simple brick masses and the elegant spacing of its windows and string courses still give

this simple structure great dignity. That 1951 fire gutted the top two stories. I got there just in time to see the whole central tower crash down into the middle of the building. All that was left were the outer walls and the original post and lintel framing of the first two floors. In the reconstruction, a new concrete frame was put inside the brick walls for support. The walls had bowed in during the fire and contractors pushed them gently back out, saving the original brickwork. Today all that is left of the original West College are those outer walls. I'm of the opinion that it would make sense to take the ivy off of them so they could be better preserved, but I have been fighting a losing battle over ivy for about 60 years. Ivy being synonymous with education is, to me, nonsense.

It is possible to rationalize the unusual subtleties of West College by trying to find the origin of the design. We know that the majority of the original trustees of Eph Williams' will, and of Williams College, went to Yale, so it is possible precedents for Williams buildings can be found at Yale. We know that East College of 1798 was a direct copy of a building at Yale.

Think about West's window panels. Yale's Connecticut Hall had a pair of windows on both ends, then a column of windows over each of the two doors, and then five columns in the middle. West at Williams differs only because it had to have doors in the center to accomodate the unusual sidewalk traffic through the building. Otherwise, the design is a simplification of Connecticut Hall at Yale, the only survivor of that college's "old brick line."

Southeast corner

"I have been fighting a losing battle over ivy for about sixty years."

*From the west
(WCMA, Currier/
Valois Lith., c. 1830)*

*Connecticut Hall
at Yale (The Yale
Library, Woodcut,
Bowen, 1786)*

East College

1798

In 1795 the enrollment at Williams was 77 at the College and 40 at the "academy", the sucessor to the free school. It became clear to the Trustees that another building was needed, a dormitory, not a multipurpose structure like West. The Trustees voted in 1796 to proceed with designing and building East College, to be placed on the eastern eminence, putting the College's only two buildings facing each other across a slight valley. East College was planned to be considerably larger than West, 104 feet long as opposed to 79 for West. It was to be four stories high, long and fairly thin, and, according to the records of the Trustees, "exactly like South at Yale," which had been finished in 1793.

Work began in 1797 and was finished in 1798. The money for construction came from the sale of two parcels of land in Maine that had been given to the College by the Commonwealth of Massachusetts.

The accompanying watercolor shows the new building on the right with the rest of the town in the foreground and on the left. The Mohawk Trail is in the distance. The watercolor, discovered in the library at Trinity College in Hartford, Conn., and given to the Williams art department, is a wonderful record of the way Williamstown looked after 1798 and before Griffin was built in 1828. It shows the original lots and some early houses (from the 1760s) in the foreground with other houses at the top, just in front of East, and more, across the street, of a later vintage –18th century.

East College was primarily for student housing, although it also had recitation

From the west (WCMA, anon. water color, c. 1800; gift of Trinity College)

.A part of the easterly vie

VILLIAMSTOWN *seen from the fourth story Old College.*

rooms for junior and senior classes. The plan shows that the interiors of both South at Yale and East at Williams revolve around fireplaces. The major rooms all have a fireplace. Occupants slept in small bedrooms that ran along the outer walls. East had two doors like Yale's South, evident in the photograph of East and in the depiction of Yale's "brick wall" (the building on the left is South). Once again, a Yale building had inspired the Williams Trustees.

The new building also had a small apartment for Albert Hopkins, the astronomer. The Adelphic Union, the literary/debating society, met frequently in one of the recitation rooms. This was a fine, massive structure with a hip roof and dormers and two doors with windows spaced evenly across the facade. There was nothing terribly extraordinary about it except that it was big. It typified the directness, the simplicity of design, that was already seen in West.

It was built like West: thick, brick, bearing walls with a wooden frame holding up the structure and the roof. It was not fireproof, though, and an enormous fire destroyed it in 1841 while the students were attending chapel services in the Congregational Church in Field Park, near the present Williams Inn. The fire was thought to have started when some coals were swept into one of the bedrooms. The building went up in an enormous conflagration and the loss created a real housing crisis. The College set out immediately to build a new East College and another dormitory, South College, as well.

Yale, South College elevation, floor plan (Trumbull, 1793)

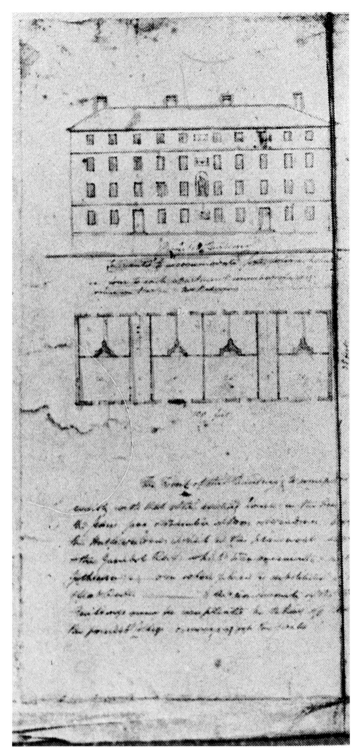

*Detail of previous
watercolor shows
the first East
College.*

*Yale, South College
(Doolittle, 1807;
Holden,* Yale: A
Pictorial History,
plate #31)

Interlude:
The Federal Style

1790's –1830's

The President's House, across Main Street from West College, is an outstanding example of the Federal style of the late 18th and early 19th centuries. It was built in 1801 by entrepreneur Samuel Sloan as a wedding present for his daughter. In 1858 it was purchased by Nathan Jackson, a friend of the College, and given to Williams to be used as the home of College Presidents.

The main characteristic of the Federal style is its elegant decorative quality, seen around the doorways and upper central windows, in the elaborate balustrades and in the giant, relatively flat, pilasters that animate the façade. Federal style roofs tended to be low, making the balustrade and the chimneys more important. One of the main practitioners of this style was Charles Bulfinch, whose major buildings are in Boston. An important example of his work is the central section of the State House. Bulfinch designed many Federal houses, as did Samuel McIntire whose work can be seen in Newburyport and Salem. The ornamentation is very delicately carved and relatively flat. The style had its origin in the work of the Adams brothers in England, who had been influenced by the then recently discovered ruins of Pompei.

The President's House has an elaborate central door with lights on each side with slit windows. Bulfinch's usual style is seen in the Palladian window: a rectangular central window sash flanked by two narrow windows centered above the doorway and topped by a decorative oval panel. This panel has a fascinating story. No one in Williamstown had the tools to carve so intricate an ornament, so it

Detail of façade, Sloan House

was made in the Boston area, went by ship to New York and up the Hudson River. It was then brought over the Taconic Trail by oxcart to be attached to the house. It contains a rather overly obvious iconography of two hearts connected by a chain, symbolic of the union of the daughter for whom the house was built and her new husband.

There are two other Federal Style houses on Main Street: the former Williamstown Public Library, and a private residence on the corner of Main and Southworth. It was owned by the College for several years in the '70s and '80s and known as Dewey House.

*Sloan House, home of
Williams presidents
since 1858*

*McIntire, Pierce-Nichols
house, Salem (Carnegie
slide collection, c. 1782)*

Griffin Hall (The Brick Church)

1828

The year 1821 was both a bad news, good news year for Williams. The bad news was the exodus from the campus of President Zephania Swift Moore with some of the faculty, some of the students and, as myth would have it, some of the library books. In fairness to President Moore, he had argued with the Trustees when he became president, saying that Williams really should be located in the Connecticut Valley. He was unilaterally carrying out that idea.

The good news was the appointment of Edward Dorr Griffin to succeed Moore. Griffin immediately set the College on the right track. He raised money to build a chapel: $10,000 would be enough to build a multi-purpose building, with its most important element a new chapel, and have some left over to establish a professorship of rhetoric and moral philosophy. Griffin had been a minister in New Jersey and in Boston, and on the faculty at Andover Theological Seminary with the wonderful title of Professor of Sacred Rhetoric and Chairman of Pulpit Eloquence. With a title like that you can go a long way.

Griffin himself was the real designer of the new building. He was familiar with Bulfinch's architecture in Andover and had copies of illustrative books by the Greenfield architect Asher Benjamin, books which were used as guides by master builders all over New England. The first thing he did was change the Trustees' plan to locate the new building near East College. Griffin selected a spot on the north side of Main Street, across from, but not in line with, East. The building would sit almost as high as East and parallel to the street atop what later became known as "Consumption

From the east (Warren, 1865 WCA)

With two original doors and 1845 addition, right. (WCA)

From the south

Bulfinch Building at Andover, 1818 (Carnegie Slide Collection)

Hill." (In 1904, to make room for a new chapel, the building was moved 40 feet to the northeast.) The bulding is dominated by a tower with a gold dome that came directly out of Asher Benjamin. Griffin called his building "the brick chapel." It was renamed in his honor in 1859.

The location presents a dramatic flank façade to the street in a bold, forceful statement. A projecting pavilion in the middle is flanked by slightly recessed wings. A pediment over the central pavilion leads up to the tower. This design feature is very similar to Andover's Bulfinch Hall. There were two doors in the façade, on the extreme left and right of the pavilion. The left hand door provided direct access to the chapel; the other, access to a small hall and stairwell that led to classrooms. Including classrooms in the building was Griffin's acknowledgment of the teaching side of the College.

In 1904 the façade was changed. The two doors were bricked up, and a central doorway put in. This was a terrible mistake by the architect, John Oakman, class of 1899. The new door has nothing to do with the Federal style. It looks more like Williamsburg than Williamstown. In March 1933, I was driving Frank Lloyd Wright to the Williams Inn and he remarked: "Who put that damn door on that quite nice building?" A fascinating question, especially coming from Wright.

(Incidentally, Wright was coming down with a cold and I had to get him some pre-World War I brandy, a fairly difficult assignment in the wake of Prohibition. Karl Weston, class of 1896, came to the rescue. He found some brandy in his attic, which I presented in a tumbler to Wright while he was in a tub in the old Williams Inn. He told me to sit down on the WC and we would talk. We chatted and later that night, in a costume of his own design, he gave a rather strange lecture to a fairly large crowd in Chapin Hall.)

The interior of Griffin Hall clearly relates to specific designs from the Asher Benjamin book. The tower is obviously his, as is Griffin 3, the so-called "faculty meeting room," which was originally the chapel. Originally a high altar on the west end had stairs leading up to it and a Palladian window above it.

(The Palladian window has been used to death in houses all over the United States. We see an example in the Bulfinch building at Andover, which President Griffin obviously knew of because he taught there for quite some time. It is clear that the ideas of President Griffin, especially about interiors and central spires with gilded domes, came from the Federal style work of Asher Benjamin.)

The chapel room had balconies on two sides, as Griffin 3 has today. The original design follows one of Benjamin's illustrations, with side aisles and piers holding up the balcony. When the room was changed to a library in 1904 this original design was destroyed. Recently the room has been restored, put back close to its original state. It's a nice interior space and is just what President Griffin wanted a single, unencumbered space.

The building is a combination of Benjamin and Bulfinch ideas, yet different from either. Our most famous early-19th century building is, in my opinion, clearly the result of the extraordinary thinking and endeavors of Griffin.

President Griffin (WCMA, c. 1821, Waldo {1793–1861} and Jewett {1789–1874})

"Our best building – our worst doorway"

ABOVE LEFT
*Griffin 3,
looking west*

ABOVE
West wall

*Design for a
Meeting House
(Asher Benjamin,*
The Country
Builder's
Assistant,
Plate 33, 1805)

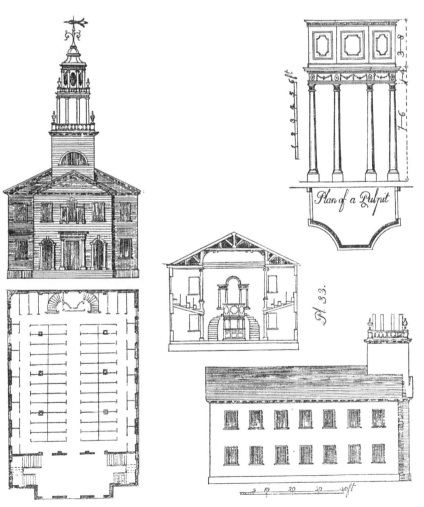

Planning

1828

Planning, as we know it today, usually involves thinking in terms of the organization of spaces in relation to roads, to views and to orientation. The early plan of Williams College was really much simpler. The Trustees decided to turn a school into a college and to build it on two eminences. They started on the western eminence, building West College there between 1791 and 1793. Next they constructed East College, on the other eminence, finishing in 1798.

In the accompanying lithograph, the two buildings face each other across a gentle valley, occupied by a cow, where Spring Street would eventually be developed. This is an example of very low-key planning. At Yale, on the other hand, early plans show brick buildings in a line animated by the lycea (libraries where the student groups gathered). Yale's formal brick-line plan was adopted by Amherst and Dartmouth.

However, Williams was off to a totally different start. The difference is quite obvious when you consider the placement of Griffin's "brick chapel," first vaguely planned to be somewhere east of East. As a new President he said that the new building should go on the high ground across the road from East, not running north and south, as were West and East Colleges, but east and west, so it faced the southern path of the sun. Its golden dome is eye-catching, and that is exactly what President Griffin wanted. He wanted a monumental building that stood out, that wasn't related to other buildings, and that would make a religious, as well as a secular, statement proclaiming the importance of Williams College.

OPPOSITE
Hand-colored lithograph (WCMA, Kidder, c.1830)

OPPOSITE
Yale's brick line, lithograph (Yale University Library, Holden's Yale: A Pictorial History)

Hopkins Observatory

1837

Hopkins Observatory, finished in 1838, was the product of research by Albert Hopkins, class of 1826, the younger brother of Mark Hopkins. He went to Europe in 1834–35 to study European observatories and to buy books and instruments. He came back full of enthusiasm and said that Williams was going to surpass Harvard and Yale in astronomical research. The building which resulted is famous as the oldest college or university observatory in the country still in operation.

It was placed near East College where students had piled stones quarried from East Mountain. Two photographs here show it in its original location. In the 1850s it was moved south, to the end of the Berkshire Quad. In 1960 in was moved again, to the north end of the same Quad.

The center of the building is an octagon with two square wings. It has heavy, quarried stones on the corners and those with a more rubbled texture in-between. On top of the stone octagon is a wooden octagon capped by a circular casing for the telescope. The original entrance is an elegant Federal doorway on the north side. The originally undecorated south door has been replaced by one similar to the north door. This is a lovely little building that has great consistency and repetition of shape.

It cost just $2,075 to build, which Albert Hopkins and several other individuals contributed. The College gave back $1,200 of Hopkins' money a couple of years later.

Another Albert Hopkins-inspired octagonal building was nicknamed

With students, 1859 (WCA)

"Two octagons, two squares and a cylinder"

The Hermitage. A "magnetic observatory" built in 1842 near what is now Driscoll Dining Hall, it was to be used for "ascertaining and exhibiting the laws of terrestrial magnetism." Before it was torn down it was used to house a student (undergraduates slept in all kinds of buildings). The octagonal shape was important from the 1840s through the mid-19th century, made famous, I think, primarily through the architecture of Thomas Jefferson. Jefferson's first house, *Bremo*, was octagonal. (To be consistent, his outhouse was also octagonal.) This well-known shape appears again at Williams in a later building, namely, Lawrence Hall.

*From the south,
in present site*

FAR LEFT
*Original north
doorway*

LEFT
*The 1842 Magnetic
Observatory (WCA)*

East and South

1841–1842

In 1841, while students were at chapel services in the Congregational Church at the head of Main Street, the 1798 East College burned to the ground in a spectacular fire, necessitating the very rapid construction of a new East, smaller than the original in all dimensions. It was to be only three, instead of four, stories, perhaps motivated by the notion that in case of another fire students might have a better chance to survive a jump from a third story window than one from the fourth floor. (Of course, the decision might have been dictated by the financial condition of the College at the time.) The new East was built in a hurry and very simply. A flat roof replaced the original's pitched roof, for instance.

East was built over the ruins of its predecessor and was aligned with its new companion, South, on a north/south axis, perhaps a first Williams reference to the brick line at Yale. The architecture is extremely simple with no elaboration. There were simple headers over each of two doors entering from the west, just as in the old East College. Its neighbor, South, is a replica of East except with a doorway on the north end.

The simplicity of West, Old East and Griffin, continued into the 1840s. The print here shows West, South and East behind the Hopkins Observatory and Griffin, right, from the southeast.

Wood engraving after a drawing by J. C. Clapp, 1844

OPPOSITE
East from the northwest, 1876, with South on the right.

"Simplicity continued"

Part Two

Nineteenth Century
Revivals
1846–1900

Goodrich
(WCA, c. 1865)

Lawrence Hall

Thomas Tefft, 1846–1847

Lawrence Hall is the first Williams example of what can be classified as a "revival" building, where earlier architectural styles are utilized by the architect in the design. In this instance, classical elements such as brick pilasters on the corners visually support a vaguely classical entablature, consisting of architrave, frieze and cornice. The interior contains elements of the Greek Ionic Order. Thus, this building is the first at Williams, with many to follow, which employ earlier styles.

Four very intelligent people conceived and built Lawrence as the first College library. This is a fascinating story which must include a little bit of background of the four.

Amos Lawrence, who gave the money to build it, was a close friend of then Williams President Mark Hopkins, class of 1824. They became friends when Lawrence, hearing Hopkins lecture in Boston, arranged to meet him. Lawrence first contributed to the rebuilding of East in 1841 and, as their friendship grew, it gave Hopkins the opportunity to say that what Williams really needed was a library.

They contacted the third member of the group, Charles Jewett, the distinguished librarian of Brown University and later of the Library of Congress. Jewett had traveled extensively in Europe and become acquainted with the centrally planned libraries that were being built in France. He had become a specialist in library design.

The fourth individual was Thomas Tefft, a sophomore at Brown and a draftsman in a Providence architectural firm, later to become an extremely

"Our first professional architect was a sophomore at Brown"

The original building (WCA)

OPPOSITE
Elevation and Section and Floor Plans, by T. A. Tefft (The John Hay Library, Brown University)

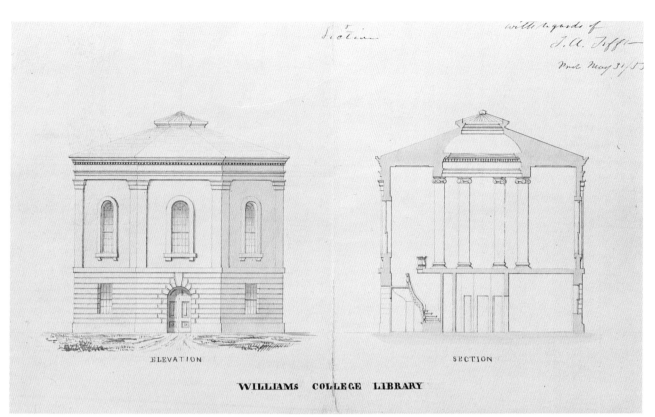

ELEVATION

SECTION

WILLIAMS COLLEGE LIBRARY

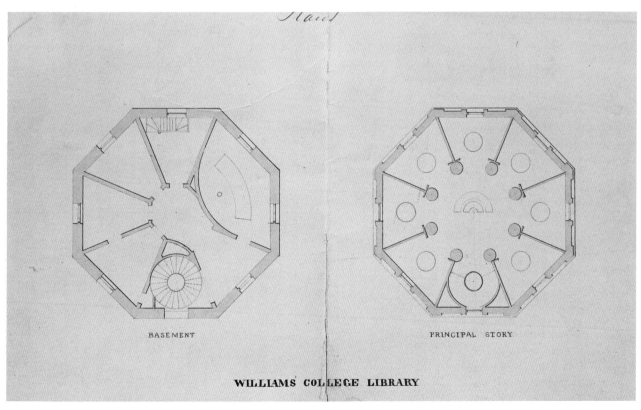

BASEMENT

PRINCIPAL STORY

WILLIAMS COLLEGE LIBRARY

important architect whose designs would include the railroad station and roundhouse in Providence. He was hired to put Jewett's ideas on paper.

The four collaborated to create an extraordinary building. The octagon is a shape already seen at Williams in the magnetic observatory and in the central core of the Hopkins Observatory. Lawrence Hall came from this tradition but had to be adapted to a much smaller scale as Mark Hopkins had made the statement that the library should be built to contain only 30,000 volumes, a number he considered "all the books that the institution is ever likely to want."

The building was a pure octagon, with nothing jutting out, and had a lookout dome over the top. The exterior has an entablature at the cornice level and a rusticated brick base. On the corners are buttresses or brick pilasters. The plan shows the two floors divided into pie-shaped elements with bookshelves radiating out from the center where the librarian sat. With a swivel chair he could look down each one of the trapezoidal shaped alcoves. (This afforded very good control if you're worried about what happens to books.) Incidentally, the library was only open two days a week. Its only purpose was to lend books. The only "reading areas" were in the spaces left over from the alcoves.

There were all sorts of preliminary designs. In one, the dome broke out of the roof a little more than it does today; in another, metal catwalks would have provided access to book storage up in the superstructure. But in the end it was simply a series

Portrait of Amos Lawrence (WCMA, Chester Harding, 1846)

The Rotunda, as a library (WCA)

of alcoves with bookcases extending back into them. The ground floor was primarily for storage, although the largest room there was the periodical room which was also used for Trustee meetings. Incidentally, that area now houses the main clerical services of the Williams College Museum of Art.

A very fascinating set of new ideas are presented here in a building that makes a strong statement. Indeed, Emeritus Professor William H. Pierson says Lawrence is the earliest example in the United States of a style called Rundbogenstil that originated in Munich in the middle of the 19th century and would spread across this country in many buildings. The Lawrence interior has elements of Greek Revival, certainly in the columns with their voluted capitals, but the exterior introduced a new German style to these shores. This building reflects the inspiration of an extraordinary group of people and it exists today as part of the Williams College Museum of Art.

Town and Gown

1850

The mid-point of the 19th Century is a good time at which to pause and look at both the campus and the town. In two paintings given to the College by the Rev. Charles Jewett Collins, class of 1845, at the end of the 1840s, we see that most buildings were built of brick. Jewett had returned to teach at Williams and obviously adored the College because he commissioned these two paintings for presentation to the College.

The first picture is the view from the middle window of the top floor of West College looking east. You can see where the footpath goes down to the gym and back up the hill beyond. It's all there today. Go up and look out that window. Seen in the painting is Griffin as it was in 1838, the "new" East and South (1841–1842) with Lawrence, just finished in 1847, in front. Visible above them on the right is the top of the Hopkins Observatory. On the left is the spire of a Greek Revival Methodist-Episcopal Church, later partially demolished. The top part was moved south and placed on a brick substructure to became, on the bottom, offices of a lumberyard and, on the top, a theater used by Cap and Bells for productions, for town voting and as an opera house.

Down the road, over Consumption Hill and across the river, there is a cloth factory, the first intrusion of the Industrial Revolution. Strangely enough, the painting does not show many farms. There were, however, a great many farms and the economy of Williamstown in mid-century was very dependent on cows which provided cheese and butter, as well as milk.

Anonymous photo looking northeast in the late 1800s. Roofs of Spring Street buildings can be seen on the right with East on the hill above. (WCA)

OPPOSITE TOP
Williamstown, looking east from West College (WCMA, anon., c. 1846)

OPPOSITE BOTTOM
West College, looking west from Griffin (WCMA, anon., c. 1846)

In the foreground to the right is Spring Street where simple, modified Greek Revival houses had replaced those of the Federal style. They were very plain, kind of temple-fronted wooden masses, with little thin pilasters on the corners, as seen on the right of the painting. On the left are some of the town's more formal homes. These were 18th-century structures, not Greek Revival, but remnants of earlier construction. On the far right-hand one sees the evolution of industry. A factory, a grist mill and saw mills that used the Green River for power.

The other picture looks west from in front of Griffin with people strolling on Main Street sidewalks and West dominating the western eminence. In the distance is the old Congregational Church where students attended chapel services. That was at the end of Main Street in what is now Field Park across from the Williams Inn. The design, Federal style, is obviously out of the Asher Benjamin book.

The lithograph shows Spring Street from the south. The condition of Spring Street in the spring was, well, treacherous. You could get stuck there. In the middle of the foreground is a low-lying building that was the second gym. To the right of that is the only outhouse I've been able to identify in any picture of the campus, a result of the prevailing thought that one should not depict them. These views also show the domestic scale of the houses.

These prints provide a good look at the town and the College at mid-century and the beginnings of the commercial side of the community.

Northeast from the foot of Spring Street (WCA, Lith., c. 1853)

Spring Street in mud season

Griffin H.

Lawrence   *East*   *South*   *Observatory*

Gym   *Outhouse*

45

Goodrich Hall (Chapel) and Alumni Hall

Gervase Wheeler, 1859

The first construction after the middle of the century was a much needed new chapel and alumni hall. Enrollment had risen and the brick chapel in Griffin was overcrowded, And the Society of Alumni, formed in 1821, was eager to have a meeting room on the campus. Gervase Wheeler, a well-known Gothic Revival architect, was hired to design this chapel/alumni hall combination.

The site chosen was on a little rise between East and the ravine sloping down to Spring Street. The interesting change is the move from brick to stone. Incidentally, with the building of Goodrich, the name of the "Brick Chapel" was changed to "Griffin Hall."

Goodrich is Gothic Revival and is, as we will see in subsequent buildings, part of a Revivalist Movement that made the second-half of the 19th century so fascinating and sometimes even funny. The façade of the church is very well organized. There is a repetition of shapes, in the windows themselves and in the way they fit into the whole triangular organization of the façade. The stone is a local dolomite coming from John Sherman's limestone quarry two miles west of Williamstown.

Wheeler got a little carried away when he designed the tower. Showing off his knowledge of all kinds of arches he went from a slightly pointed arch, to a flat arch, to a pointed arch, covering the whole vocabulary of arches as he built his spire. An entrance in the base of the spire let you into both the alumni hall and the chapel.

Goodrich (WCA, c. 1865)

"A handsome Gothic Revival"

Incidentally, this chapel had to be enlarged later on in the century by adding a west transept. Indeed, the whole building is now, as we will see later, a student-run campus activities center.

Everything in the well organized interior flowed together nicely, culminating with the organ above the altar. The whole interior was simply done in dark wood with pews that would hold the entire student body. As a whole this church displays extremely well coordinated architectural form. Only the tower is a slight aberration.

Goodrich, with East, South and Lawrence (WCA, c. 1883)

Interior of the chapel (WCA, c. 1865)

Bascom House

1865

Bascom (WCA, Warren, 1865)

An exuberant eclecticism overtook the campus in the latter part of the 19th Century. Examples of this include the Gothic Revival Goodrich, and the Bascom House on Park Street and a third marvelously eclectic building which no longer exists, the Field Memorial Observatory.

Bascom House is Gothic in form with all sorts of stained glass and multiple mullion windows. Built as the home of a member of the Williams faculty, it has all the trappings of Gothic reduced to wood and glass.

It has the same steeply pitched roofs, multiple pointed arches and stained glass windows seen in the Goodrich Chapel. Although privately built, Bascom was owned by the College from about 1960 to 1980 and used at various times for faculty offices, student housing and headquarters of the Center for Environmental Studies. It returned to private ownership and has been beautifully restored and preserved.

Field Memorial Observatory

1880

Field Observatory in The Knolls (WCA, c. 1882)

The Field Memorial Observatory was a fabulous structure on the southern edge of the campus, and it represented another, quite specialized, kind of revival. It used all sorts of architecture as inspiration. Basically North Italian Early Renaissance, it had small engaged pilasters, small Corinthian capitals, and exuberant paneling on all surfaces. More to the point, it was made of cast iron. Everything you saw in this building, all of the detail work, came from a mold.

The use of cast iron for the building of first bridges and then buildings was augmented in the 19th century by the designs of James Bogardus. Eventually, with the invention of the Bessemer Converter, cast iron could be turned into steel, leading us to the creation of today's skyscrapers.

However, the use of cast iron for buildings, especially store fronts, was very much in style at this time and cast iron buildings could be ordered from cata- logues and shipped all over the country. In fact, they were delivered to the west coast by boat, making the trip around Cape Horn.

The Field Observatory had a major problem. It rattled in the wind. It evidently was almost impossible, unless you had a very still night, to make any calculations that would be accurate. Functionally it was a flop, but it was a wonderful structure, and it's too bad that it wasn't preserved.

Morgan Hall

J. C. Cady and Co., 1882

Morgan Hall is another marvelous example of the exuberance of the eclectic revivalism which dominated the second-half of the 19th century. Built in 1882, it was designed by J. C. Cady and Co. of New York City. This firm was very popular in the 1880s and 1890s and designed many buildings for Vassar and Trinity colleges and quite a few buildings in New York City.

Morgan was the first campus building to be connected to a College heating plant. It had central heating (no more stoves). It was also the first dormitory to have plumbing, including indoor bathrooms. There were six large bathrooms and an equal number of water-closets in the basement. Bathing rooms, according to the 1883 Anthneum, were "at the disposal of all the occupants once each week."

Running water had been brought into some of the other buildings but for the most part outhouses were still the order of the day. The opening of Morgan in 1883 was a Williams celebration of modern technology. Even then it wasn't until 1905 that toilets were added on each floor, necessitating cutting new windows at the ends of the dorm and adding additional dormer windows in the rear of the center section. Electricity was brought into the building at the same time.

(This brings up the point that flush toilets would not work unless there were all sorts of valves that kept the sewer gases from coming back up and killing the person above. It was the inventiveness of a very fascinating Englishman named Thomas Crapper which made the flush toilet work and there is an interesting book by him called *Flush With Pride: The Story of*

Thomas Crapper. He invented this system and designed many quite luxurious toilets with animals supporting the bowl and so forth. His name appears on the back of the bowl, "Thomas Crapper." That name was recognized by World War I soldiers in England and is why some of the words have relevence today.)

The architecture has always appeared to me to be a combination of Jacobethan and Elizabethan – long, rather large, masses with quite a few windows and wings and a wonderfully ornate superstructure. Morgan was all

East façade

"A strong statement, sort of Jacobethan"

built out of the same stone as Goodrich, dolomite, so that it balances the campus. The details show a relationship to structures in England and the elaborate shape of the dormers has overtones of buildings in Flanders, especially those in Brussels. There is one little detail that shows up on each end as a kind of conical hat shape – almost a Chinese paddy hat. But on the whole the building is massive and strong.

Morgan is a huge wall running east to west, and together with the Lasell Gym, with its tower, creates a dramatic gate for Spring Street.

From the northwest

Restored Gargoyle above northwest doorway

Lasell Gym

J. C. Cady and Co., 1886

The Lasell Gym is basically Romanesque. The architect, J. C. Cady of New York City, trained with a German architect who seems to have schooled him in the German treatment of the Romanesque Revival. The general impact of the Gym is of a centrally located mass accented by a tower on the corner over a doorway. This tower anchors the building. Together with Morgan Hall, the gym serves as a gate to Spring Street.

The major massing is dominated by a low lantern which rises above the roof. The interior of the basketball court is lit by clerestory windows. The Gym's material is dolomite, a local stone similar to that used in both Goodrich and Morgan. Lasell anchors the stone core or center of the campus, with Goodrich on the east and Morgan to the west. Surrounding buildings, with the exception of Hopkins across the street, are brick.

Rows of windows set in relieving arches animate the mass along Spring Street. It's a strong statement, somewhat different from Morgan, but just as powerful.

The interior is of interest because of the design of the basketball court. This building was built in 1886 and basketball was not invented until 1891. The placement of the structural supports around the outside of the main floor held up the roof but sure didn't contribute to the good health of the basketball players.

Lasell was added to and in the process changed considerably in 1928 when the main gym roof was raised, making possible a better basketball court. The building was also extended south and southeast to provide facilities for other athletic endeavors.

TOP
Construction photo showing clearstory (WCA)

OPPOSITE
View from northwest, shows changes to roofline resulting from the 1928 renovation.

ABOVE
Decorated for Class of 1915 junior prom, Nov. 13, 1913 (WCA)

"Together with Morgan, the gateway to Williamstown"

Hopkins Hall

Francis Allen, 1890

Hopkins Hall, designed in 1890 by Francis Allen of Boston, continues the Romanesque Revival seen in the gym but now quite differently handled by a Richardsonian architect. It reflects the influence of Henry Hobson Richardson, one of America's greatest architects who designed Trinity Church in Boston and the Allegheny County Courthouse and the jail in Pittsburgh. He was America's first national architect. Unfortunately, Richardson had died in 1886, so Hopkins was designed by someone trying to emulate him, and this made a big difference.

The characteristics of Henry Hobson Richardson are preserved but sometimes not quite as successfully combined into a whole as Richardson would have done. From the southwest, it is dominated by a circular tower that is embedded into the mass of the building, which has a "presidential bulge" in the bottom. The middle area housed the Treasurer of the College, and above that was a corner classroom. This created a wonderful sequence – president to treasurer to a classroom containing a plaster copy of the Winged Victory (I enjoy the symbolism – president to treasurer to Victory).

Hopkins is a very massive building, and when you look at it head-on from the south, it is perhaps somewhat overbearing. It has too many different materials. Stonework combined with a special, relatively long, brick, creates visual confusion.

The design is clearly in the style of Richardson, but from a point of view of quality, not quite as good. Dormer windows, corner towers and strong

From the southeast

"Looks as though it has been squeezed in a four way vise"

West entrance

stone molding separating the courses are hallmarks of Richardson's work. The detail of the west doorway (serving at the time as the main entrance because it faced into the campus and opened onto an access road) shows very low springing; probably Richardson's interpretation of early Christian churches in Syria. Work about them had been published in great detail about the time he was designing his buildings.

The interior had high ceilinged rooms and some wonderful details which are now gone because the building was totally gutted when an addition was put on in 1987–88. The 1987 detail of the stairwell shows you some of the Richardsonian interest in metal.

(I suggested at a Faculty Meeting once that you needed another tower on the right corner as you face the building from the south because that would symbolically represent the provost and the dean, who were not represented by anything except a right angle turn in the wall. Of course you'd have to have a function for that tower. I suggested that it could be filled with old, no longer needed, computer print-outs and, after so many years when it would be full you could light them and heat the building for a whole winter. However, this suggestion didn't go over well with anybody.)

Richardson was famous for his railroad stations, for his libraries, and for many wonderful houses, both in stone and in wood. In Hopkins Hall we have a taste, but only a taste, of a Richardson building.

*Third floor art
history classroom
(WCA)*

*Stair railing
(TWB, 1987)*

*"Only a taste of
a Richardson
building"*

Thompson Scientific Laboratories

Francis Allen, 1892–93

In 1892–93 the Thompson Scientific Laboratories were constructed in a line running east-west along land south of West College. The buildings were built separately, but subsequently have been connected with extensions, additions, and, recently, a new entrance to a huge scientific complex running along their south walls.

The three original buildings are, from east to west: Physics, Chemistry and Biology. Their architect was Francis Allen who had just designed Hopkins Hall.

The buildings are not as Romanesque as Hopkins. They tend to be a more simplified sort of Georgian, with limestone lintels above the windows and simple, round-headed doorways. It is interesting to see this row as it lines up making the southern east-west boundary of the lab campus. There is nothing extremely distinguished about the buildings except that they have served a great many students for a great many years in their three disciplines.

TOP RIGHT
Physics, Chemistry and Biology, from the northwest (WCA)

RIGHT
Laboratory (WCA, c. 1904)

Jesup Hall

George Tilden, 1899

The donor of this building – Morris Ketchum Jesup – was very active in the evolution at Williams of the Young Men's Christian Society, the YMCA, which become the Williams Christian Society here in 1908. He paid for the building because he wanted to see a place for students to develop on their own.[1]

Students had urged the construction of a campus center devoted to their "social and religious welfare." Jesup and College officials envisioned it as "a place to integrate the multiple aspects of campus life incorporating student group offices, athletic offices and trophy display areas, a sophisticated performance space, a sizeable reading area, accomodations for 10 students, a well equipped billiard room and a generous amount of space for the religious groups."

The auditorium/theater played a major role in Jesup's desire to improve the whole life of Williams undergraduates. Elected society officers lived in the building which was often referred to as "the YMCA" despire its varied uses. It even had a room for the Mandolin Club. Later on there was a Gargoyle suite.

As outside activities increased and the administration grew, Jesup began to house practically every facet of the Williams administration. The President never used it, but the Alumni, Development, News Director and Alumni Review offices were there until they moved to the former Theta Delta Chi house (Mears House) in 1983. At one time the head of Buildings and Grounds had a basement office there. Many student

From the north-west (WCA, a pre-1908 postcard)

Oakman's 1908 façade (WCA)

organizations, The Record, The Gul, the Williams Outing Club., were here until rooms were built for them in Baxter Hall.

The narrow stage of the theater was the home, when I was a student in the 1930s, of The Little Theater, a student-run operation. Of all the plays we produced the one which was the most fun was Gilbert and Sullivan's *Cox and Box* with music: Professor Charles (Tommy) Stafford, class of 1892, pounding the piano. You had to be careful in staging plays because stage right would only hold five people.

This auditorium was a great room for debates or lectures. Buckminster Fuller talked for two and a half hours non-stop in the 1950s and the hall was always filled.

I think George Tilden's design created a wonderful, if highly idiosyncratic, building. It picks up just enough of the character of the three Thompson science buildings that are at right angles to it, so that it fits in and forms the eastern boundary of the science quadrangle. We're using that term "quadrangle" in a very loose way. This is not an Olmsted quadrangle with four closed sides. This is an "open," Williams-style quadrangle.

Jesup was built of bright orange brick and had an elaborate superstructure with dormer windows and chimneys in quite a Baroque manner. A simple doorway with a round arch was surmounted by an elaborate stone tablet.

In 1908 this design was totally changed by John Oakman, class of 1899, who had gone to Paris after graduation and studied at the Ecole des Beaux-arts. He became an "expert" on the architecture of the world, and totally dismembered this building, Colonializing it, and basically emasculating it. He changed the middle section by putting a big Palladian window over the doorway, adding a whole new entrance with columns. He basically destroyed what I thought was a very exciting, somewhat different, design.

(I might point out that he is the same architect who added that 1904 doorway to Griffin Hall which has no relationship to the construction year, 1828. It shouldn't have been added, a fact I already said Frank Lloyd Wright mentioned in 1934.)

Jesup had been a stunning building, one that didn't need to altered, didn't need to have have its roofline regularized, and certainly didn't need a big Palladian window. Jesup's original intriguing character was dimmed considerably by these changes.

[1] A great deal has been discovered about this quite remarkable building and it appears in a Winter Study paper by Ryan Mayhew '01 who was working with Professor of Art Michael Lewis. Mayhew's paper on Jesup is available in the College archives.

OPPOSITE TOP
Before 1904 renovations (WCA)

OPPOSITE BOTTOM
The "new" stage treatment (WHT, 1967)

"A wonderful, if highly idiosyncratic building"

Part Three

The Revivals
Continue
1902–1961

Thompson Memorial Chapel from the northeast

Olmsted letter

April 28, 1902

In 1902 the College hired the Olmsted brothers of Brookline to help choose a site for the Thompson Memorial Chapel. The pair responded to President Henry Hopkins with a long and detailed letter going beyond their original charge to offer some sweeping reactions to the College's architecture and location. The Olmsteds greatly admired the Williams environment, the views of the mountains, and the trees. They liked Williamstown so much that they argued that the President and Trustees should change Williams to a three-year college with the students staying through the summers so they could enjoy all four seasons in the Berkshires.

The Olmsteds came to the campus with a lot of architectural and planning lingo and baggage and they had a virulent case of quadrangle-itis. They couldn't conceive of any campus without lots and lots of closed quadrangles, an idea based on the Oxford and Cambridge models used by the Ivy League colleges. Of course, most of those campuses were in cities or large towns where the tendency was to look inward rather than outward. Another idea that was fixed in the Olmsted brothers' minds was that a college should be built of only one material, of one color.

When the Olmsteds arrived they found an extremely mixed bag. There were no quadrangles and practically every building was built of a different material and in a different style. The only planning, or anything that could be called planning, were the decisions to put West on the west eminence and East on the east eminence. Griffin had not been aligned with either. When East burned in 1841, a new and

Clark, 1882; Observatory, 1838; South and East, 1842; Lawrence, 1847 (WCA)

Goodrich, 1859; Lasell, 1886; Morgan, 1882

smaller East and a second dorm, South, had been aligned, reflective of Yale's "Brick Line." Just to the east were three randomly located buildings of different materials. Hopkins Observatory, 1837, was stone and wood and located near the edge of what is now the Berkshire Quad. The Natural History Museum, over in the southeast corner of that area, was built of brick. At what is the present quad's northeast corner, where Currier now sits, was the first Clark geology building, built in the 1840s. This was a sort of Romanesque structure which would gain the distinction of having had (in 1896) a wall collapse.

To the west they found Lawrence Hall (the 1847 brick octagonal library version), the stone Gothic Goodrich and then two other major stone buildings the Lasell gym (1886) and Morgan Hall (1882). They didn't like Morgan because its east-west orientation neces-

sitated having some rooms on the north side, a concept they found objectionable. They missed completely the subtlety of Morgan and Lasell working together to form a kind of wall, with a gateway between looking south into the town's business district. Their dissatisfaction with Williams was epitomized by the 1890 Hopkins Hall with its different colored stone and different kinds of brick.

They approved of the alignment of the Thompson Scientific Laboratories and even mentioned that a building off Hoxsey Street would begin the process of making a quadrangle, an idea that would come to fruition 50 years later with the construction of the Bronfman Science Center.

They had a problem with the Congregational Church, then not the most attractive Romanesque brick structure with two non-matching

steeples on the south end facing the town across Main Street. That structure is still there, inside the clapboards of the present church building, with the towers replaced by the typical single New England spire. They suggested it would be nice if the College owned that land so that a quadrangle could be planned there. They also suggested moving the President's house to create a massing of buildings. Fortunately none of this came to pass.

Their first choice of a location for the new Chapel was between Lawrence and Griffin, right in the middle of Route 2. They would have divided the road to create an island in which the chapel's façade would be to the west and the choir to the east. Their second choice was where the Faculty Club now is but that was too close to the Episcopal Church, which they found much too rustic.

The site questions were finally

answered by the gradual deterioration of the Goodrich Hall gym between Hopkins Hall and Griffin Hall. That Goodrich was a quite remarkable and not uninteresting Gothic Revival stone and wood building with lots of fascinating pointed arches that made it look as though it was a book hanging from its spine with the pages fanning open. The sciences were in the basement and the building groaned and shook so that people using that area felt they were in danger. The college decided to take it down, shortening its already endangered life to make that central site available for the Thompson Memorial Chapel.

They had mentioned a quadrangle with one side open toward Main Street, which is what we have with the East Quad and the area in front of the Museum (Lawrence Hall). When the Olmsteds were here the campus had a stone central core, a brick line of science laboratories, West College wandering around by itself, and the brick line of East and South with an extraordinary unplanned mixture on the east side. Perhaps their ideas of some kind of order were good and I think, as you will see in the later discussion of the East Quad, had some effect in how that quad was designed. This did not keep the College from changing architects, thinking in terms of different materials, nor did it convince Williams to make the campus uniform and very dull like some colleges I won't mention.

I fear the Olmsteds didn't realize how much the surrounding mountains meant to faculty, students and alumni. Solid quadrangles tend to shut off views, denying the excitement of seeing between buildings. At Williams we want to see the mountains. "O, proudly rise the monarchs of our mountain land . . . we greet them with a song," as Washington Gladden said.

*Hopkins Hall,
1890; Thompson
Chapel, 1904;
Griffin Hall, 1828*

Thompson Memorial Chapel

Allen and Collens, 1904

At about the same time as faculty were reporting that the Goodrich gym, an 1859 building with a gym on the top floor and sciences in the basement, was making queer noises, Mary Clark Thompson offered to build a chapel for the College as a memorial to her late husband, Frederick Ferris Thompson, class of 1856 and a frequent College benefactor. Deciding that the old Goodrich was indeed becoming dangerous, College officials ordered it demolished and moved Griffin Hall to the northeast, clearing the way for the construction of the Thompson Chapel. It is English Gothic Revival. Although Francis Allen was the senior partner of the firm, the chapel is probably mostly the work of Collens, a new member of the firm recently out of architectural school and with access to perhaps too many books on English Gothic.

As you look at it from the south the tower dominates. I have moments of wanting to have the tower lie down and the church stand up. The tower is based on a church in Wells, not the cathedral, but St. Cuthbert. If you compare the Thompson tower with St. Cuthbert (right) they are almost identical. The tower stands at the southeast corner and anchors the chapel on the site. Thompson has a low mass on the south side which contains the narthex with a small entrance porch on the southwest corner. You enter the narthex, which continues on into the tower but you turn left through three doors to get into the interesting but somewhat confusing interior of the church. It is a squarish space, in sections, with thin aisles flanking it. The nave and aisles lead to a crossing with shallow transepts on each side, and finally, in the northern section of the building, a raised chancel.

Wells, St. Cuthbert, England (WCMA, anon.)

OPPOSITE
South façade

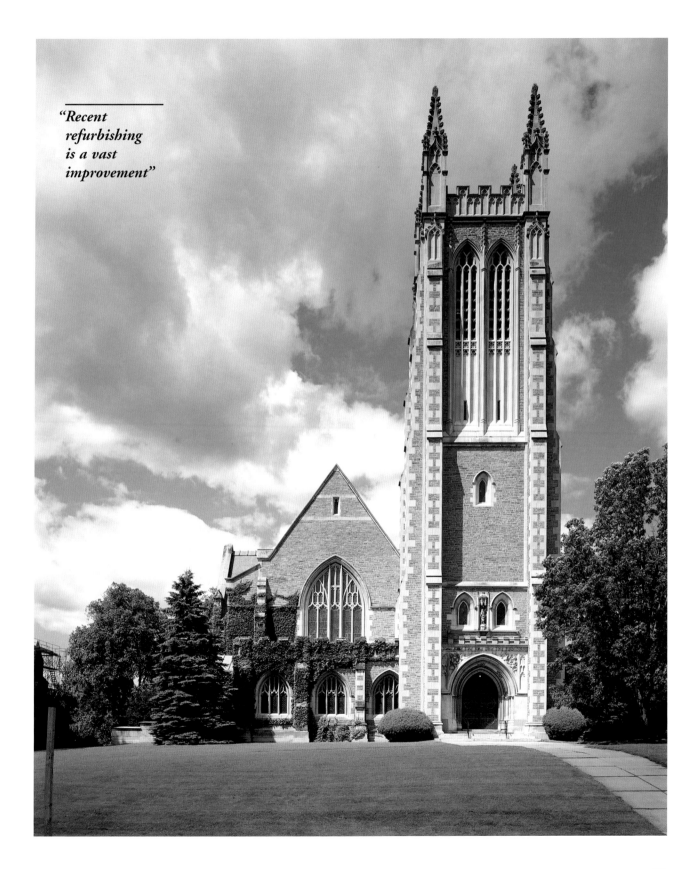

"Recent refurbishing is a vast improvement"

So there's a sequential series of spaces leading you to the chancel.

The building was dedicated by Mrs. Thompson "to the glory of God" and the memory of her late husband. The College would expand on the memorial concept later when it honored alumni who gave their lives in military service in wartime. The main hall has memorial plaques for deceased veterans of World Wars I and II as well as the Korean and Vietnam conflicts.

marvelous job of unifying the spaces. At the same time, spot lighting has improved visibility of the big plaques that list those lost in the various wars.

The interior space was at its best in June of 2000 at the reunion memorial service. The chapel was filled with people, the organ was wide open, the alumni chorus was growing hoarser by the minute, and the Dixieland band playing, very loudly, *The Saints Come Marching In*. Nothing

LEFT
Nave and main aisle

RIGHT
Choir and east transept

The chancel contains furniture for the choir and an organ console. The space has been greatly helped recently by new lighting. The lighting in the nave was originally bare light bulbs around the top of angels carved in the spandrels of the nave arcade. These Edison light bulbs, a kind of precursor of Oldenburg in many respects, have been removed and some very handsome fixtures have been hung that greatly improve the whole space, to say nothing of the lighting. These suspended lights, through both the transept and the crossing, do a

else has quite filled the chapel with the sound of music as this curious ensemble of musicians.

The marker indicating that the grave of Eph Williams is located in the basement of the chapel has been moved from the floor in front of the choir to a wall niche at the right and it looks great there. This relocation, the new interior lighting and the installation of the Korean and Vietnam memorial panel on the south wall of the nave were funded by a Class of 1950 reunion gift.

The East Quad

1905–08

"A true Williams quadrangle"

Currier   *Fitch (Berkshire)*   *East*   *South (Fayerweather)*

The Williams administration reacted positively to the criticisms in the 1902 letter from the Olmsted brothers, objecting to a lack of planning on the campus and to the wide variety of construction materials used in the buildings. So, as the College grew in size and more student housing was needed, the whole emphasis shifted to bringing some order out of chaos, particularly in the eastern section of the campus that was filled with buildings in odd positions. On the east quad there was of course the Hopkins

Observatory wandering around in the middle space, not really related to anything. Jackson Hall, a Natural History museum, was located in the southeast corner (it was torn down in 1908). In the northeast area was Clark Hall, the first Geology building, which had partially fallen down in 1896 and was finally torn down in 1907-08. With these buildings gone, it was possible to make a kind of loose, Williams quadrangle, a quadrangle that doesn't have its corners filled up but is open to views of the mountains, the mountains

The quad looking south from the Chapel tower (WCA, c. 1912)

RIGHT
*Fitch from
the northwest*

BOTTOM
*East from
the northeast*

**"Some vague
planning is
evident here"**

having a very strong impact on anything done on the campus.

The first of the new construction, in 1905, designed by Allen and Collens, was Berkshire Hall, now called Fitch House, on the southeast corner and an addition on the south end of South College, which was renamed Fayerweather. The southern section of the quad is established by these two north-south buildings. That set off a kind of rumble which resulted in new doorways being added on both sides of East in 1907. The idea was to coordinate the whole quadrangle by giving all of the buildings doorways with columns.

Fitch is a very handsome building with two doorways that have columns on each side in Colonial Revival format. It is a three-story brick building that is quite handsomely animated with limestone. Across the quad in Fayerweather, the new construction had to go downhill on the southern end, over the brow of a hill, so that on that end it is four floors, not three. The addition contained some student "duplexes" – two-story apartments. It was called the "Gold Coast" because it was a little fancier than any other student housing. (That all changed when both East and Fayerweather were gutted and concrete prefab interiors installed in the 1950s.)

The northeast corner remained empty, and it is there that our friend Oakman designed a new building, Currier. This is a handsome building, intended to be a center for the non-fraternity students. It had a palatial living room, now converted to bedrooms, on the entrance floor. You go down, as the land slopes to the east, to a dining room with small living rooms off it to the north. This space

Fayerweather from the southwest (WSS)

OPPOSITE TOP
Currier from the southwest . . .

OPPOSITE BOTTOM
. . . and from the east

had a different life when it was the temporary home of the music department for a few years until the new music center was dedicated in 1979. The quad, as you can see in a view taken from the tower of the chapel, makes a quadrangle that has spaces between the buildings.

When the Hopkins Observatory was moved south in 1908 and placed on a raised platform, Williams had its first real quadrangle. While not an Anglican quadrangle, as in Oxford, Cambridge or Harvard, this is a true Williams quadrangle, identifiable yet offering views of the surrounding mountains.

Clark Hall (Geology)

Frank Wallis and William J. Rogers

1908

This relatively small, rectangular building replaced an earlier Clark Hall which had been situated near Prospect in the Berkshire quad. Located in the Science quad, it is perpendicular to the north-south axis of West College and parallel with the line of the three Thompson science buildings of 1892. It demarks the northwest corner of the science quad. The north side of the building marks the edge of the town right-of-way.

The main door, on the northeast corner, is a classical entranceway with double columns and an entablature emphasized and capped by a Palladian window. Located in a lobby just inside is a plaque listing the donating members of the family of Edward Clark of the Class of 1831 (including Robert Sterling Clark who built the Clark Art Institute) for whom the bulding is named.

On both the north and south sides of the building central sections are slightly recessed. Each of the projecting end sections has a vertical tier of windows capped by a Palladian window. This is basically a very lovely building. It's not trying to say too much, and what it says, it says elegantly.

"A nice, small structure with a plethora of Palladian windows"

TOP
From the northeast

ABOVE
From the south

Williams Hall

Cram and Ferguson, 1911

The building of two dormitories was a strategic part of the plan for this section of the campus, adjacent to Chapin Hall. Williams, finished in 1911, came first and Sage was built after the war in 1923. Both are elongated L-shaped structures, with the short parts of the L's nearly meeting on the west to form a gateway onto Park Street. This creates a partial quadrangle open to the east, facing Chapin.

The architecture of Williams Hall is not at all the simple architecture of West and Old East or even similar to the new East and South. All of these were simple brick buildings. Williams is much fancier. It has its three stories divided by string-courses of limestone. It has an elaborate door in the west end and only slightly less elaborate doors across its inner courtyard side. The L-shaped mass is divided into five entries with individual staircases. A fourth floor features elaborate dormers.

Architecturally speaking, Williams Hall is more Georgian Revival than the other campus buildings. The formal Georgian Revival of Cram and Ferguson is evident in the quoining, the elaborate interlacing of projecting brick layers that emphasize the corners of the building. The doorways are Baroque portals with pediments above them and engaged pilasters. On the north side of Williams, in a 1990s renovation, the College excavated the land to put windows in student rooms in what were originally central basement bathrooms – a very sensible reutilization of space.

TOP
From the south on spring weekend (WHT, 1966)

ABOVE
From the southeast

Chapin Hall

Cram and Ferguson, 1911-1912

With the construction of Chapin Hall, the College moved into quite a different era of building. There was an internationally known architect in Boston, Ralph Adams Cram, who could switch quite dramatically between Gothic Revival and the Georgian of James Gibbs. The selection of this important new architect to do the work on Chapin resulted in the contributions needed from major donors for construction. Then the question was where the building should be located. An undated plan which Cram drew addressed this problem and is a fascinating look at the kind of planning that Cram followed – everything carefully worked out.

The Chapin Hall that was built takes its name from the donor, Alfred Clark Chapin, a member of the Williams class of 1869. It was first called Grace Hall to honor Mrs. Chapin. Unfortunately Grace died in 1908. Mr. Chapin remarried in 1913 and in 1920–21 the building was renamed: Chapin Hall.

The façade is wonderfully large-scale and majestic with six oversized Indiana limestone monoliths that arrived in Williamstown on special rail cars from the Midwest. Chapin is the only building on campus that has real big monolithic columns. The portico façade has a pediment above it in High Georgian Revival style with brick and limestone trimmed quoining and elaborate doorways. The result is monumental and really stands out when you walk the long haul north from Main Street. It is similar in many ways to the façade of the Senate House in Cambridge, England, a centerpiece there. The Senate House provided a large open space for the conferring of degrees.

Senate House, Cambridge, 1721–30 (Friedman, James Gibbs, *plate 253)*

OPPOSITE
From the south

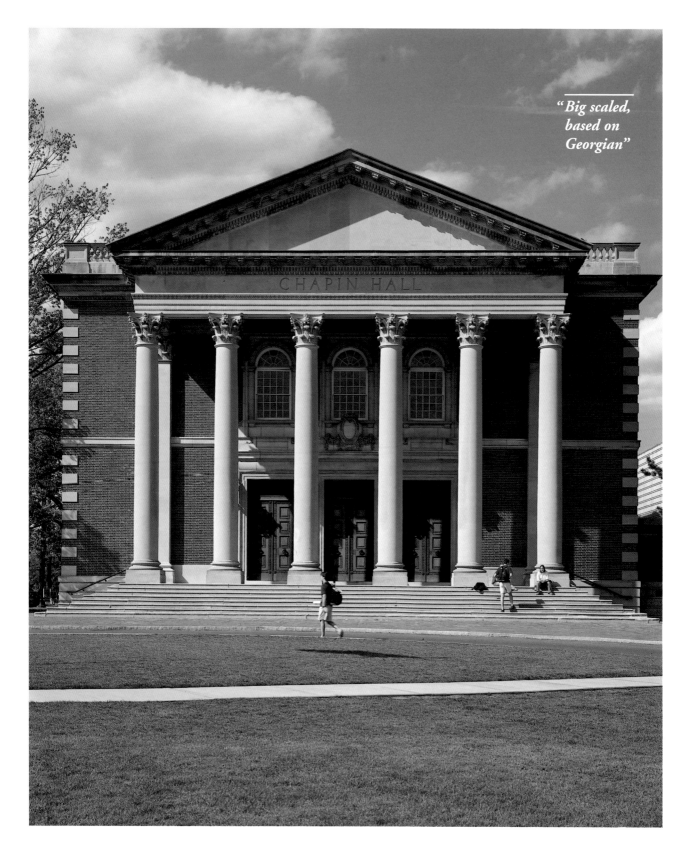

81

The interior of both Chapin Hall and the Senate House are large rectangular spaces with seating on the sides facing in. It is clear that the design of Chapin follows closely the design of the Senate House. The inclining seats on the sides are identical; the balcony is very similar. Everything is nearly the same except that the ceiling is bowed in Chapin and flat in the Senate House. The fenestration is similar and so are the details of the lovely woodwork and the stucco of the ceiling.

In Chapin the floor declines slightly to a stage at the north end. This stage, incidentally, before the building of the AMT, was used for plays. I remember one in 1934, *Aristophanes, the Clouds*, performed by Cap and Bells with a producer from Broadway. I remember it because I was one of 15 "clouds" up on a teetering platform cantilevered out from the balcony and covered with tulle. We were singing fake Greek music that was written by Professor Tommy Safford.

TOP LEFT
Chapin's interior today

LEFT
Senate House, Cambridge, England (Friedman, James Gibbs, *plate 254)*

OPPOSITE
Convocation (WHT, 1966)

Thompson

Allen & Collens, 1911

TOP
From the west

ABOVE
Doorway (WSS, 2000)

This infirmary, given by Mary Clark Thompson, is a lovely small building. The major part of the house is the infirmary with solaria on each end. A wing on the back contained rooms for people with infectious diseases. The main part of the building is a rectangular mass capped by a gambrel roof with dormer windows.

This structure has a lot of subtle refinements. The doorway, for instance, has a handsome metal and glass canopy protecting it. This is the last Williams building done by Allen and Collens. They started in 1890 with the Richardsonian Romanesque of Hopkins and in 1892–93 did the three Thompson Scientific Laboratories in a kind of modified Georgian style. Then they did the Chapel in 1904 and Berkshire and Fayerweather in 1905. This building served the College as an infirmary until 1986 (when a new health center was built at the end of Hoxsey Street) although a portion of it began to be used for student housing in 1980. Since 1986 it has been all dormitory space.

I had two not-so-sharp experiences in this building. In one I was recovering from a ruptured appendix in 1938 (before the era of sulfa) and later, after a skiing accident on Sheep Hill, from a broken and dislocated shoulder. So I got to know the operating room in the cellar (which would be condemned a few years later). In that room Dr. McWilliams, who had to operate in a tent in World War I, took out my appendix over Thanksgiving vacation in 1938 and Dr. Coughlin worked on my shoulder.

Sage Hall

Cram and Ferguson, 1923

"A mirrored version of Williams"

Sage Hall has the same floor plan as its neighbor, Williams, but flopped over, using the same L-shape with separate entries. The ends of the bases of the L's almost meet, so these two buildings, with Chapin Hall on the east, form a loose quadrangle.

For many years there were tennis courts to the immediate south of Sage that were flooded in the winter for hockey. (The hockey action moved to the pond below the Cole Field House in 1933.)

Perhaps Williams and Sage Halls lack some of the directness and simplicity of the College's earlier buildings, but they are certainly in the spirit of Chapin and perhaps that of the 'teens and 'twenties in the country.

Tennis Courts   *Sage (1923)*   *Williams (1911)*   *Chapin (1911-12)*

TOP
From the northeast

ABOVE
*Freshman quad
with tennis courts
(WCA, c. 1925)*

85

Stetson Hall

Cram and Ferguson, 1923

From southeast showing original stacks (WCA, c. 1945)

OPPOSITE TOP
From the west

OPPOSITE BOTTOM
From the southwest

Stetson Hall satisfied a tremendous post-World War I need for a new College library. Lawrence Hall (1847), as had been suggested by Mark Hopkins, only held 30,000 volumes. With the rebuilding of Griffin in 1904, some bookshelves had been added in the faculty room, but even with that, library space was grossly inadequate. Fortunately, at that moment, the College had two big donors. One was the previously mentioned Alfred Clark Chapin; the other, Francis Lynde Stetson of the class of 1867. Their contributions made it possible for the College to build a new library building and to include rooms for the Chapin Rare Book Library.

The architecture is an example of the Georgian Revival style of Cram and Ferguson at its finest. The major façade faces west and the stacks are on the

"Distinguished building – needs careful mothering"

*Reference room
(WCA, c. 1930)*

east. Inside there are two masses. On the right (south) side, on the second and third floor is the Chapin Library, one of the most distinguished rare book libraries in the country. The left (north) side contains a large, two-story room that housed a reference library and reading room. There are offices and a few classrooms on the top floor. Fireplaces were situated in strategic places throughout.

The exterior involves dramatic quoining on the corners of the building and an arcade above the west entrance-way that contains nothing, but catches

snow and leaves. It does, however, provide a fine place for wandering, especially at receptions in the Chapin Library. The upper, indented part of the building is similar to the garden facade of the Pitti Palace in Florence.

The doorway on the south side, like those on Williams and Sage, is very elaborate Georgian baroque. It leads into what was the main circulation room in the center of the ground floor. Books were stored in the stacks to the east. These stacks are structural, holding up marble floors which provide access to the various levels.

The two-story main reference room is a very handsome, vertical space with lots of light from above and woodwork similar to that in the interior of Chapin Hall. It's a very lovely room which, with lots of bookshelves, could provide suitable storage for items from the archives or even the Chapin Library, perhaps giving it a whole new life. Indeed, there is great potential in this whole building which has been added to a couple of times and now contains offices for many of the College's faculty members as well as the College archives.

The Chapin Library is a lovely space with secure storage for its extensive holdings, a safe for manuscripts and a large area for exhibitions. The centerpiece of the Chapin is an elaborate display case which holds the four founding documents of the United States: *The Declaration of Independence*, the *Articles of Confederation*, the *Constitution*, and the *Bill of Rights*. The Chapin Library and the National Archives in Washington are the only two places in the world which have all four documents on permanent public display.

Chapin Rare Book Library

Cole Field House

Densmore, LeClare and Robbins

1926

From the south

RIGHT
Lower Cole fields from the southwest - Pine Cobble in the background (TWB, 2000)

This building was constructed on a rise overlooking the Cole Field athletic fields and two ponds. The area is extremely busy in the fall and spring with men's and women's sports including football, soccer, field hockey, softball, lacrosse, and, at the very eastern end, men's and women's rugby clubs, which have very active memberships. Almost half of the Williams students, 49 percent of them, compete in intercollegiate athletics. As most of the fall and spring teams use this building and its surrounding fields, the number of students involved here is quite extraordinary.

Below the Field House, to the north, are the two ponds, of one which used to serve as the home ice of Williams hockey. The athletic fields are at two levels. The women's lacrosse field and the football practice area are slightly lower and the raised section to the east houses the other sports. This creates a wonderful kind of bowl, particularly spectacular during the fall foliage season, with Pine Cobble, and The Dome overlooking it.

The building is essentially a locker/dressing room structure housing showers and amenities for both Williams teams and visitors. Consequently there is a tremendous amount of plumbing in the building and this has been updated several times. The basement is used for training rooms and storage and there is an attic that once was used as sleeping quarters for members of visiting teams.

The building is sort of Georgian with relieving arches containing windows. There are dormer windows on the top floor. A portico at the center is sort of skinny, but it is O.K. While it looks kind of fragile, it fits in with the building.

In 1926 the Trustees thought they might make this building part of a new gym, situated near the athletic fields. But in 1928 they made the wise decision to expand Lasell Gym to the east and southeast and to include new basketball courts and a larger pool. Keeping the main athletic facility in the center of the campus and the town was a good idea.

Lasell Extension

Densmore, Leclare and Robbins

1928

Just before the debacle with the stock market and the upcoming Great Depression, the College met a shortage of athletic facilities by building a large addition to Lasell Gymnasium using the same architects who had just finished the Cole Field House. At one point consideration was given to developing a new gym complex on Cole Field, but instead College officials decided to add to the 1886 Lasell Gym and completely rebuild the north end, raising the roof and getting rid of the piers around the outside of the basketball court and adding an indoor track on a balcony around the court. A new wing, to the south, contained a swimming pool with two floors of rooms above it for wrestling and a second basketball court. Locker rooms were enlarged and the gym was brought up to date.

The exterior of this addition is quite interesting because the architects from Boston respected the original gym by Cady and Company. They used the same stone – dolomite from local quarries – and they used the same shapes in the relieving arches and windows. The fenestration was kept the same and, very important, a new square doorway led to the pool. The handsome new Spring Street facade echoes the east side of Morgan. These architects were obviously conscious of the role of Morgan and the Gym in creating a kind of gateway to Spring Street.

TOP RIGHT
From the west showing the 1928 addition (WCA, Kinsman, 1929)

RIGHT
Addition from the southwest

Lehman Hall

Cram and Ferguson, 1928

"Back to the simplicity of West"

The major donor to the construction of this building was New York Govenor Herbert Lehman, class of 1899. The architecture is of interest because it is a simplified Cram and Ferguson design. It would seem as though either Govenor Lehman or the architects rediscovered West College, Griffin or the simplicity of East and South (before they were ornamented in the early 20th century) and returned to the simplicity and directness of those earlier structures.

Located behind Chapin (and the later Bernard Music building), Lehman is at the north end of the main campus but is related laterally to the nearby Williams and Sage Halls. It is a two-entry structure with living room/bedroom suites opening off the first and second floors. There are single rooms on the third floor. It was planned to have a similar building to the east with steps between them. Although the staircase is in place, the second building was never constructed.

ABOVE
From the southwest

RIGHT
Southwest entrance

Squash Courts

Shreve, Lamb '04, Harmon, 1938

The year 1937-38 wasn't a very good time to build anything. The Depression was still very much on and the war clouds were getting much darker in Europe, but build the College did, and with the help of quite a few alumni added a new sport into the Williams athletic offerings. After all, you can't play squash on a macadam sidewalk.

We have a problem with the exterior. The grey concrete block, the material used in the exterior walls of the courts, is quite different from the dolomite stone used in the 1928 addition to the original Lasell gym.

Space was left between the 1928 addition and the squash courts, although the two were connected by a tunnel at the basement level. There were two floors of squash courts in the main structure. Each floor had six courts. In addition, in an eastern section there was a doubles squash court and two others for singles. Those two singles courts were the only ones that had any kind of seating capacity for spectators.

These courts turned out to be very fine, fast courts and a whole new era of very good squash followed. An exciting new sport was added to the athletic curriculum. Incidentally, the architects are better known for their principal work: the Empire State Building.

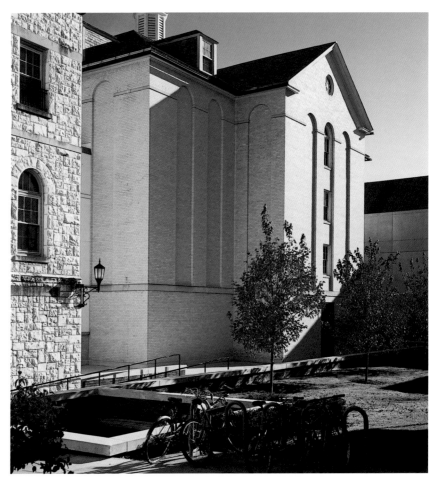

From the northwest

New landscaping (1998)

"Architecturally unrelated to adjacent gym

Faculty House

T. H. Ellett, 1939

The Faculty House was dedicated in January 1939. The gift of Clark Williams, class of 1892, and his wife Anna, it is located on the corner of Park and Main Streets, in line with the President's House. It was originally planned to have one entrance for women and one for men, but that archaic idea was never realized.

The building is a simple Greek cross with a lovely living room in the center and two porches with pediments – one on the east and one on the south. The kitchen is on the first floor with staff living quarters and two guest rooms upstairs. The club has many things that are associated with the "gentleman's era." It has, for instance, a billiard/pool room, a card room and a pair of bowling alleys in the basement. The exterior has a sort of a clubbed Monticello look, as though someone had hit Monticello over the head with a big flat sledgehammer.

The two-story living room is very handsome with an elegant wooden ceiling. While in 1938 the College faculty needed housing more than a fancy new club, the building was given to the College, and, with a later addition (as I will discuss later), has fulfilled its function extremely well.

From Main Street

Living room – portrait of donor over fireplace

"This looks like 'Clubbed Monticello' – but it's nice

Heating Plant

Ralph Adams Cram, 1934

In 1933 and 1934 there was a great deal of discussion on the Williams campus about the design proposed by Ralph Adams Cram for a new heating plant. Both students and faculty were involved in this debate which centered around the basic question of whether or not the College should build a Georgian heating plant. The students made their voices heard in *The Williams Record*. The faculty spokesmen were professor Karl E. Weston, class of 1896, and assistant professor Andrew Keck, class of 1924. They represented the entire art department and were very vocal in speaking and in writing letters to Cram questioning the use of high Georgian architecture for a college heating plant. The two professors pointed out that quite a lot had happened in the world of architecture in recent decades, noting especially the work of Louis Sullivan and Frank Lloyd Wright. They thought that it was rather strange to be building a Georgian heating plant when there were many different and more modern approaches to the design of buildings.

Letters were exchanged between the professors and Cram and, if my memory is correct, the design was simplified. The building you see today does not have the original's giant pilasters or engaged Corinthian columns, which I remember. It was finally built, as you see it today, quite simply, although it does have an attic story that doesn't express anything on the inside and it uses string courses of a different material in a kind of reduced Georgian variance. It is of interest, that at the same time Williams voices were questioning a Georgian heating plant, questions were being raised at Yale about Gothic

1934 Heating Plant (SS, 1947)

1902 Heating Plant now a B&G garage (WMW, 2000)

quadrangles and at Harvard about
Georgian residential houses.

The heating plant was altered in 1953
when the south wall was torn out in
order to get a new piece of equipment
in to help convey coal directly to the
boilers. On the north, an addition in
1970 accomodated a new kind of fur-
nace which now does most of the work
in heating the campus. There is one
footnote: at one point there was a
contractor who came up with a purple
brick with which to build the heating
plant. This was turned down –
probably a good thing.

**"Overly elaborate;
caused quite a stir"**

Adams Memorial Theater

Cram and McCandles, 1941

The story of the designing and building of the Adams Memorial Theater is bizarre. Katherine Adams Wells came to Williamstown to meet with President Phinney Baxter to talk about what she might want to give to the College. The subject was made public immediately because she was very deaf and had a huge ear trumpet into which Phinney had to yell. A series of discussions followed:

Mrs. Wells asked, "Do you have a museum?"
Baxter, yelling, replied, "Yes!"
"Do you want an administration building?"
"No, we have one!"
Finally she said, "Do you want a theater?"
"We would love a theater!,"
the president answered.

So the Adams Memorial Theater was born. The architect in charge was Ralph Adams Cram. He did the first design himself and it was strange! I studied the plan with Max Flowers, the director of the theater. What Cram had done was take the main auditorium of Chapin and duplicate it to make the theater. Then someone reminded him that he needed a 99-foot tower over the stage on the north end to hold lights and suspended scenery. In the auditorium he had piers between inclined side and center seating sections, effectively destroying sight lines. Someone had mentioned that we ought to have a proper home for the Paul Whiteman Collection, so he repeated the Chapin Library on top of the entrance. The result was a strange looking building that didn't work, and was rejected.

As a new design was started, it was decided it might be a good idea to consult the people at the Yale Drama School. Stanley McCandles of Yale got

us on the right track. His suggestions led to an interior design of a functional theater – one that worked – with an auditorium with walls curving to the proscenium so that sight lines would be unobstructed.

The two main emphases were the stage with its framing and the auditorium, as seen in the plan, with an entrance way with rooms on the sides. The floor, ceiling and walls of the auditorium converge to create a frame for the proscenium. The play ends up being the thing that unites the two major masses – the vertical tower in which all the scenery is held and the horizontal interior space which holds the audience.
The exterior was still evolving. Some elevations included elaborate Roman arches across the front leaving no place to put the words: "Adams Memorial Theater." They were thrown out.

Architectural drawing of the design first accepted by the Board of Trustees

OPPOSITE TOP
From the southwest

"A fascinating building with a convoluted history"

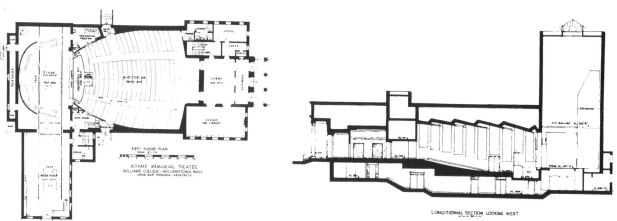

FIRST FLOOR PLAN

ADAMS MEMORIAL THEATRE
WILLIAMS COLLEGE · WILLIAMSTOWN, MASS
CRAM AND FERGUSON · ARCHITECTS

LONGITUDINAL SECTION LOOKING WEST

The auditorium
(WCA, c. 1950)

Finally, the people at Yale suggested stepping the building up in a series of simple masses, as you can see in a design that was accepted by the Trustees. The masses in this modern design stepped up in two sequences: entrance to projection booth, and auditorium to stage tower.

One problem, however, remained. The yellowish stone which had been designated was going to be too expensive, well above the $250,000 budget. In the process of changing to brick, more designers in the office of Cram and

Ferguson got loose and the building became essentially Georgian, with a pedimented front that is actually more Greek than Georgian. The modern exterior was lost. The pedimented portico was the same height as the second mass, so there was no stepping up in a sequential and interesting fashion.

And then, evidently, the tower bothered trustees and architects alike so they decided to put limestone stripes all over the exterior. The final design loses the sense of a sequence of forms and ends up with stripes in all kinds of places

The Trojan Women
(CL, 1999)

trying to make the 99-foot tower look smaller. The trustees thought the new front portico would reflect that of the recently completed Faculty Club.

In the end you have a building that everybody likes more than if it had been built as originally designed, but it is a schizophrenic building with a functional and handsome interior behind a façade that has no relationship to how the building functions. But as a workable theater, it is excellent.

The plan and the longitudinal section show how it was constructed. Indeed, the longitudinal section shows what happens when a roof is placed on the pedimented front, spoiling the climbing up of the masses to the tower. This is a fascinating building with a convoluted history. It is unfortunate that it couldn't have been built as originally designed. We had a chance to construct our first modern building and now would not do so for another 20 years.

101

Alumni House (The Log)

Kenneth Reynolds '16, 1941

In November of 1941 an important event in Williams history took place, namely the dedication of the College Alumni House. A small group of alumni had discussed acquiring a building where alumni could gather before and after football games, and throughout the year, to picnic and meet, to sing and, indeed, to dance. The project was started by getting the College, in the person of Charles Makepeace '00, the treasurer of the College, to give this group the use of a house on Spring Street to be the Alumni House. This house had a living room and a small first room after its entrance way, and an upstairs with bedrooms and a bath. It was an instant success. Over the following years a series of additions extended it to the east and it was put on one of the tentacles of the College heating plant.

The house was decorated with some murals and a bar was installed along with storage lockers. The building eventually became a student pub, "The Log," because the alumni really used it only on home football weekends. This however ended abruptly when the Massachusetts State Legislature raised the minimum legal age for the use of alcoholic beverages from 18 to 21. This destroyed the function of a college pub and this was a shame.

The building now has many purposes. It still serves well alumni who drop in in the fall or spring for that matter, and it is used by academic departments for lunches. It is also once again being used by students as a kind of get-away place/coffee house. Large alumni gatherings now take place up in the Faculty House/Alumni Center.

West façade

OPPOSITE
Football game reception (WHT, 1955)

The Log, sequence of rooms

OPPOSITE
The Log, mural
Towers and
Cupolas *by Dwight Shepler '22*

The additions are interesting. One, to the back, was constructed in 1946 of wood salvaged from a North Adams mill. Another room, still further east, was built in 1952 using beams saved from West College following the fire there the previous year.

The whole space has a nice rustic feel, only somewhat marred by the necessary addition of a sprinkler system. All and all, The Log has been a very successful building and it functions well for all kinds of informal gatherings.

Over the years a wonderful sequence of bands has appeared there, starting with Heine Greer's Dixieland Band, led by Henry K. Greer '22, and later the Boston Jazz Band led by Bill Payne '32. Both played regularly on Homecoming football game and Reunion weekends.

Stetson Apartments/Poker Flats

Kenneth Reynolds '16, 1946

TOP
*Poker Flats from the northeast
(SS, 1947)*

ABOVE
*Bernice Shainman at the door
of the apartment she and her
husband, Professor Irwin
Shainman, occupied. (IS, 1948)*

This building, built as faculty housing, has two names. Officially The Stetson Apartments, it is much better known as "Poker Flats."

Faculty housing was a great problem in the late 1940s, with the return of both faculty and student veterans from the war and the general reawakening of the College. Many new, young faculty members were arriving with wives and young families. Architect Kenneth Reynolds '16, who designed The Log, created a long, thin, two-story brick structure with 12 apartments. Each consisted of a living room, a kitchen and dining area, two bedrooms and a bath, plus storage. It was, shall we say, somewhat minimal, but not all that bad, and the rent was low. As I remember it was about $60 a month.

This was very popular space. It had a nice view of the mountains on the north side of the campus, and was within walking distance of the classrooms. The only drawback of the apartments was they used a structure called flexicord, precast beams that were the ceiling of the lower apartments and the floor of the upper apartments. While sound structurally, they were quite good at transmitting noise. Recently this building was converted to student apartments and was all fancied up with extra porches and doorways.

"Minimal, inexpensive housing"

Weston Field House

Peter P. Welanetz, 1951

It seems there have always been problems with the bathroom facilities on Weston Field. This story starts before 1951 when the only bathrooms were in the basement of the baseball stands, a wonderful wooden structure built in 1895. Chemical toilets were installed there, two in a women's room and one in a men's room in which there was also a funnel in the corner, for obvious purposes.

This Neanderthal situation continued until 1951 when Lindsay Dodge '24, concerned about the amount of plumbing in relation to the number of people attending home games, decided something had to be done. He offered to pay for a new structure which would contain bathrooms for men and women and team rooms for the football players, both Williams and their opponents. The result was a square building made out of corrugated metal, about as dull as could be. However, it only cost $17,500 and most of that went to connecting the plumbing to the town sewers.

Conditions were not as Neanderthal as they had been in the baseball stands, but almost. The men's room contained a trough that ran the width of the building – the women's room I have not seen but it can't be that great. At any rate, that is the situation as it exists now and I would call it maybe three quarters Neanderthal as opposed to all Neanderthal. It is likely that still more will be done to improve this uncomfortable situation.

TOP
Homecoming crowd (TWB, 2000)

ABOVE
From the southwest

"Functional, but Neanderthal"

Fire in West College

1951-2

On the night of January 2, 1951, fire broke out in the upper northern part of West College. It was during vacation so there was nobody in the building. Officials thought it was caused by an electrical problem. It burned furiously for several hours, consuming the upper two floors. West was a wooden timber framed building, and once the frame caught the fire progressed rapidly. Fire apparatus from Bennington, Pittsfield, Adams, North Adams and Williamstown responded to the biggest fire in Northern Berkshire in a good many years.

All that was saved were the four exterior walls. To repair the building, contractors built a new reinforced concrete frame and tied the walls to it. The goal of this restoration was to save as much of the brickwork as possible and it was amazing that more than 90 percent of the exterior walls were preserved.

The only problem with this reconstruction is that a new east door was installed, one which has nothing to do with the West College of 1791. Much too elaborate, it is the product of the architectural firm of Perry, Shaw, Hepburn, Kehoe and Dean which had worked very successfully with the Rockefellers in the redoing and rebuilding of Williamsburg. As I mentioned before, Williamstown is not Williamsburg.

The fire (WHT, January 2, 1951)

Interior, after the fire (WSS, 1951)

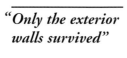

"Only the exterior walls survived"

As it is today

East doorway

Baxter Hall

Perry, Shaw, Hepburn, Kehoe and Dean, 1953

TOP
*From the southeast
(WSS)*

ABOVE
*Snack bar wing
from the south*

Baxter Hall, a combination student union and freshman dining hall, with room for limited upper class dining, was a very important structure. It was located between the President's House and the Freshman Quad, eliminating the tennis courts. It's too bad in a way that it had to be built where it is, but there really was no other site. It had to be near the freshman quad.

The firm of Perry, Shaw, Hepburn, Kehoe and Dean could think only in classical terms. Several people saw Mr. Perry of this firm making drawings of the door of Griffin Hall.

Griffin was built in 1828 but the door that he was drawing was put on in 1904 and doesn't fit with the rest of that building. The design of Baxter has been somewhat questionable from the very start.

The building has some major problems, the result of the architects not having a clear idea of the proposed use of the building before coming up with a plan for its construction. Consequently, the building really doesn't work very well. I was involved in the original design. I was asked by the Treasurer of the College to look the

plans over and write a report. I said I thought the architects should start all over. They did not and I'm sorry to say that the College has had to suffer with some really inexcusably bad planning. The part of the building that works the best is the Snack Bar. It's of interest that there was student input in the design of this area. Students had been using the Log as a snack bar, and they liked the wooden interiors and asked if wood couldn't be put in the snack bar where Baxter bulges to the south. It was and the result is quite a nice room.

There have been many transformations of parts of the building. The most successful one was the conversion of one of the living rooms into a student post office.

The exterior of Baxter has a kind of Post Modern look. It is, of course, based on the classical and one wonders why that was still being considered important in 1953. At any rate, it is named for a great Williams president – James Phinney Baxter '14 – and it serves many functions. Presently, yet another committee is studying the future of this building.

TOP
Snack bar

ABOVE
Main dining room

Lansing Chapman
Hockey Rink

Mollenburg and Betz,

1953, 1960, 1969

Hockey at Williams has been played on many facilities over the years, some of them somewhat questionable. It was played on flooded tennis courts where Baxter Hall is now located, then on a rectangular pond just below the Cole Field House, which I experienced in 1934 as a varsity goalie. I vividly recall that during that winter the temperature went down to 15 degrees below zero and stayed there for almost two weeks.

In 1953, a new rink was built east of Spring Street with boards and artificial ice. It was right near the College coal pile. That created a problem because a southwest wind would blow coal dust onto the ice causing the skaters to fall down and necessitating frequent sharpening of skates and sweeping of the ice.

In 1960-61 the rink was covered with canopy-style roof. The ends were left open and a strong north wind at a hockey game made this a super wind tunnel. These conditions often necessitated some internal use of alcohol as antifreeze.

Ends were finally placed on the building in 1969 and the entrance, lobby, rest room facilities and team locker and shower rooms were soon added. At this time the building was named in memory of W. Lansing Chapman '10 at the request of William L. Chapman Jr. '37 who, with other family members, contributed to this final stage of construction.

From the northeast (WHT, 1953)

The roof going up (WHT, 1961)

Set up for tennis (WHT, 1970)

From the southeast in 2000

Ready for hockey, from the southwest, 1999-2000

The building serves two sports: hockey in the winter and tennis in the spring, summer and fall. It's a straight-forward building, engineered with great grace and with no artificial attempt to gussie it up. I had the feeling that the baby blue paint used in the hockey rink when it was first built was sort of unsympathetic to the way hockey is played, but the interior is simple and handsome.

Taconic Golf Club

Seymour Saltus, 1955

The Taconic Golf Club, one of the finest golf courses in the northeast, had a new club house built in 1955 when the old club up on South Street was given up and the center of golfing activities was moved east toward Water Street. The clubhouse is a nice, low-lying colonial building with extensions for the living-dining room projecting to the west and several porches and patios. It's in a very convenient location and, incidentally, adjacent to Weston Field which makes it handy for halftime visits during home football games.

TOP
*Cross-country skier passes west
of the clubhouse during the
"off" season*

ABOVE
The 18th fairway (TWB, 2000)

Stetson Faculty Offices

Cram and Ferguson, 1956

In the mid-1950s, to meet a great need for more faculty office space, the decision was made to enlarge Stetson to the east, building an addition specifically to contain faculty offices. It was clear that the exterior of the addition should blend in with the old building and the architects did that well. They carried the mixed-arch treatment of some of Stetson's windows into the addition and even picked up on the occasional plain rectangular theme of other portions of the older building. Problems arose from the height of the ceilings (seven feet), dictated by the height of the adjacent old stacks of the original building. Now there is a move to redo Stetson, because of the needed enlargement of the College libraries and the need to renovate and expand faculty office space. The future of this section of the building is up in the air.

From the south

Roper Center

Cram and Ferguson, 1962

In 1946 the Roper Public Opinion Research Center was founded at Williams College. It was located in rooms in the northeastern part of Stetson Library. It was renamed in 1947 the Roper Center, which simplified things considerably. It stayed in those quarters until moving into an extensive addition which was dedicated in the Fall of 1962 with a big ceremony. This addition, offices, storage and discussion rooms, extends from the northeast corner of the library, in the general direction of the Roman Catholic Church. It's a nice direct structure designed by the firm of Cram and Ferguson, the architects of Stetson

From the east

Library, and continues its simplified Georgian style.

The Roper operation was here until 1977 when it was moved to the University of Connecticut at Storrs. At present this nice space is occupied by the Offices of Career Counseling. It has rooms for job interviews, lounge

spaces and small areas to carry out the business of the placement bureau (Career Counseling as it's called).

During an interim period in the 1980s, this long, thin structure housed the Art Department's slide library while an addition was being built on the College museum.

115

Service Building

Kirby and Welanetz, 1962

TOP
*From the south
(TWB, c. 1970)*

ABOVE
*Loading dock on east
side of the shop wing,
from the north*

The Building and Grounds Department's one-story Service Building is obviously very carefully laid out and efficiently planned. From the south, in the right-hand wing, are the main offices. The wing that goes from the street to the north towards the heating plant is where all the various service teams, such as painters, plumbers, etc., have their shops and their supplies.

A loading dock on the east side of that wing opens directly into the various shops and into the shipping and receiving space. The parking area in front of the loading dock houses the collection of vans and cars the College uses to move athletic teams and others around the countryside. The building's fenestration has recently been improved and it has become a nice, simple, structure that functions well.

Williams College Underground

Not many people are aware of it, but there is an underground college in Williamstown. It consists of tunnels that connect the various Williams buildings with the heating plant. These tunnels are very handy. They carry the heat that is supplied to all the buildings from the main heating plant. Water, sewage, electric and phone services, and the recently added computer network cables, are also run through the tunnels. These tunnels are not open to the public, but segments of the public have been known to find a way into them. Many alumni will remember them as a cool, quiet place to drink beer, etc. Now, however, it is nearly impossible to gain access.

As a matter of fact, it would have been helpful if they had been closed to the public when I was a senior. Our senior dance in the gym was a financial disaster because students found a way to get from Morgan into Lasell Gym without passing through the entrance where we were picking up the money to pay the orchestra.

With all of the services that run through the tunnels, the only thing left up topside to mar the idyllic nature of the campus is the multitude of electric and telephone wires and poles along Main Street.

_____

"Once a fashionable late-night hangout"

The tunnels (in red) run from the heating plant in the lower right, across the campus to the Dodd complex in the upper right corner and to the Greylock Quad in the upper left.

Part Four

Modern Architecture (Beyond the Angevine Report) 1962–2001

Mission Park
The dining hall wing

Prospect House

Shepley, Bulfinch, Richardson and Abbott, 1962

The planning on Prospect House began around 1960, at a time when the College was in a state of turmoil caused by the Angevine Report (implemented in 1962) which stated that the College must feed and house all students. This building was originally designed as just a dormitory, and then in the middle of the planning it became clear that it had to be considered part of a residential house system. So, on the bottom floor student rooms were omitted in favor of a library/study room and some living room space. The building reflected the transitional nature of the campus.

The exterior is impressive, whether you look at it from the north or from its more overpowering view – the south. It seems to me that the architects designed Prospect to relate to Berkshire and Fayerweather: it has the same number of stories and is brick. However, instead of having single windows, the glass is treated in a larger scale. Vertical panels of brick and glass alternate across the facade. Chimneys also function as vents for plumbing. In scale, the building fits in well with its neighbors.

Architects' rendering, from the north (1961)

OPPOSITE
From the southeast

"Our first 'non-traditional' dorm"

Driscoll Dining Hall

Shepley, Bulfinch, Richardson and Abbott, 1963

Driscoll was designed to serve the East, or Berkshire, quad and has ample living room and dining space. The basic design motif is intersecting and overlapping circles that create some fascinating spaces within the building. Since it is a concrete building, with poured concrete walls, it was easier to use curving walls. A stone veneer was added to the exterior.

The interior spaces seem to work extremely well. From either the west or the north you enter the small circle that is higher than any other mass. From that you may access directly another circular room, the living room, or a circular staircase that gets you down one flight into dining rooms in the two larger circular spaces. The food line descends the circular staircase in a way that makes wainting in line a pleasant experience and promotes conversation. The dining rooms in the two big circular masses have concrete ceilings animated by wooden rafters. A great deal of light comes in from strip windows, and from big windows separated by large areas of wall.

The living room has a continuous wall of glass going around the whole exterior wall. The kitchen and service line are away from the glass and very efficiently constructed. From the outside I think this is a very handsome series of shapes echoing each other in a nice harmony of texture and color in the stone and in the forms themselves. It is clear that the principal architect on this building, Jean Paul Carolin, owes a slight debt to some of Frank Lloyd Wright's use of intersecting circles and octagons, as seen in some of his houses built in the 1940s and 1950s.

TOP
Construction, from the west (WHT)

ABOVE
From the northwest (WHT)

OPPOSITE TOP
From the west

OPPOSITE LEFT
Living room

OPPOSITE RIGHT
Dining room

Greylock Quadrangle

The Architects Collaborative
(Ben Thompson), 1965

With the publishing of the Angevine Report in 1962, just after the arrival of Jack Sawyer '39 as President, it became clear that the College would need more dormitory space and facilities for feeding students. Greylock came into being as a result. The residential house system in Greylock is the result of this change in the social environment of the campus, and is a fine indication of how the new Williams was to evolve.

The Standing Committee, of which I was a member, was involved in the planning of Greylock and had a role in encouraging the trustees of the fraternities to transfer the fraternity houses to the College. This procedure began in 1963. Standing Committee members made a foray to Andover to see the work of Ben Thompson, a member of the Architects Collaborative of Cambridge. Thompson showed the committee around Andover and we were impressed with their housing, their art studio building and an addition to their museum. Thompson was chosen to be the designer of the Greylock complex and was also put in charge of refurbishing the lower floor of Berkshire/Fitch to make room for a lounge and snack bar.

Planning the Greylock houses was complicated and took a long time because of the complexity of the site being used for four residential buildings, housing 288 students, and a separate dining building. The site on the corner of Main and North Streets sloped precipitously to the AMT which buttresses the southeast corner. The design problem was to situate these four residential houses so as to have them step down

RIGHT
Aerial from the north (WHT, 1966)

BELOW, RIGHT
Architect's plot map:
A *Bryant*
B *Hopkins*
C *Carter*
D *Gladden*
E *Dining Hall*

OPPOSITE TOP
Hopkins and Carter

OPPOSITE BOTTOM
Gladden

"Great buildings, superbly planned"

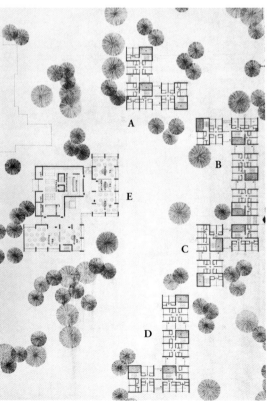

*Dining Hall from
the northwest*

Courtyard

the west-to-east slope, which also dropped off somewhat to the north.

The resulting residential houses are quite geometric in form and they dovetail, leaving lovely passages between them with diagonal paths in the center between buildings. An early aerial view shows that what the architect was doing was exactly the opposite of creating a quadrangle. He made as many of the rooms as possible face outward, toward spaces between buildings, so that views of the mountains are maximized.

The buildings have rich red brick walls capped by high concrete cornices that hide the venting quite effectively. Horizontal concrete slabs create both floors and ceilings. Inside, ceilings are waffled and contain the light fixtures.

In Greylock, students for the first time were asked what they would like to see in a new building. The President named a student committee to present ideas to the architect about how Williams students wanted to live. This committee, which I organized, had a typical dorm room built in the Lasell Gym, and the student members took turns living in it for a while. When they compiled their reactions it was obvious that they wanted a room of their own in which to study and to sleep.

Greylock rooms are rectangular or squarish, and from the last count that I have from students living there, there are 26 ways they can arrange their furniture. That's a lot of ways for individuals to express themselves. There are singles off the main corridors, and, in the connecting parts, suites with single bedrooms opening onto common living rooms.

The dining hall is strategically placed so that it easily draws students from all four dormitory buildings. The first floor of this building contains meeting rooms, lounges and class rooms, while the second floor has three dining rooms, two small and one large. The coffers in the dining hall ceilings are twice as large as those used elsewhere in this complex, creating a majestic visual scale. An especially handsome staircase connects the two floors.

The residential houses are named after poets and scholars. From south to north they are Bryant, Hopkins, Carter and Gladden – Washington Gladden, class of 1859, the author of "The Mountains." From many of the rooms you can see between the buildings and see the inspiration for his words to the song, *The Mountains.*

TOP
Dining Hall

ABOVE
Student room

Bronfman Science Center

Ben Thompson Associates, 1967

With the help of many committees of scientists, Bronfman emerged as a multifaceted building containing, in the northern mass, new homes for mathematics and psychology, with their libraries, and with classrooms on the ground floor. Below them, in the basement, there is a large auditorium. A connecting link, in the middle of the building, has staircases and lobbies and leads to the south end which houses science research labs for faculty/student collaboration.

The siting of this big building is extremely important. The architect worked with his model, playing around with the masses to adjust how they would work in relation to the available open space, bordered on the northeast corner by the Clark Geology building, on the southeast by the Thompson laboratory buildings, and, to the east, Jesup Hall.

Bronfman kind of blocks the view to the west, but spaces between buildings allow the space to ooze out as it were. Its placement makes an extremely successful, if complicated, statement at the west end of the science quadrangle.

Because of the nature of the interior, it is framed more in concrete than in brick. The architectural forms are similar to those in Greylock. All of these buildings tie in visually with adjacent buildings. The architect accomplished this through relating various levels in the buildings. A big cornice crowns Bronfman on the same level as the Palladian windows in the top story of Geology and the attic story of Biology. This creates an extraordinary sense of Bronfman having always been there.

The finest interior space in the building is the library for mathematics and psychology, being used now, since the advent of the unified science center, as a student study area. (The mathematics department was previously on the top floor of Hopkins and many of its faculty lived into their 80s and 90s, because, it is theorized, of the exercise they got going back and forth to the basement bathrooms.)

The library is a two-story room, open in the middle with a mezzanine going all around and a staircase that reflects the interior shape. The library is can-

tilevered out to the north, and that projection is sympathetic to the big window in what was once the museum of the Geology building. I think this building is extremely successful in terms of echoing parts of, and understanding it's relationship to, other buildings on the lab campus.

Bronfman is, in my mind, the finest building that has been built at Williams in recent years. Thompson, the architect, was the 1992 recipient of the American Institution of Architects Gold Medal and he did some of his best work here at Williams.

John A. Shaw Boathouse

Jonathan Rose '63, 1970

Although Williams crew has roots that go back to the golden age of intercollegiate rowing in the 1870's, it became a permanent part of the Williams athletic scene only in 1968, when a young history professor of the class of '62 , who had had a successful rowing career in Philadelphia and at Cambridge, (and for whom the boathouse is named), generated sufficient student interest to float several second hand eight-oared shells on Onota Lake in Pittsfield.

For the first two years, the crew rowed out of a boy's camp on the western shore of the lake, but in 1969, Shaw (looking for permanent quarters) found, on the opposite shore, a long, narrow building which had once been a garage for the ice wagons that annually removed the lake ice to provide refrigeration for the town. He negotiated its sale for $10,000 with a one-armed Polish slumlord from Pittsfield, and made some rough drawings which Jonathan Rose '63 (then practicing architecture in Pittsfield) turned into today's boathouse.

In addition to being head coach, Shaw served as general contractor, fundraiser and donor for the project. The boathouse was opened in the Spring of 1970 just in time for the first Little Three competition for the Saratoga Oar. The boathouse was designed to hold six eight-oared shells, two or three fours, and assorted smaller boats. The increasing popularity of the two season sport, and the advent of women's crew in 1973 have, however, pushed the boathouse's capacity to its limits. Its facilities and its setting on the spectacular mountain lake have, nonetheless, produced several generations of first

rate crews, various New England championships and Henley victories, a handful of national and Olympic team picks, and two world championships. *(Submitted by JAS)*

TOP
Moving across the ice to new location (JAS, 1970)

ABOVE
Nearly finished in time for the first Little Three Saratoga Oar (JAS, 1970)

Herbert Towne Field House

Lockwood Greene, 1970

ABOVE
The southwest corner

LEFT
Under construction showing groin vault of laminated wood with hockey rink in the background, (WHT, 1969)

The Herbert Towne Field House is a handsome building adjacent to the Lansing Chapman Hockey Rink, completed one year earlier. The field house is a fascinating engineering project with no frills. It's a straightforward structure with big laminated wooden beams creating two large groin vaults. The central beams connect with secondary ones and the roof is laid directly on top of them. All of the engineering details show and become part of the building design. It is multi-functional, used by spring athletic teams, such as lacrosse, tennis and baseball, and year-round for track and recreational walking. In one corner is a whole mountain climbing operation that scares the hell out of me. The south end is a simple wall with a large expanse of glass.

Mission Park

Mitchell and Giurgola, 1971

The 1970s opened with the completion of a large building, Mission Park, on the north edge of the campus. It was conceived as a wall separating the central College buildings from the Cole athletic fields. The building is essentially a four-story structure that undulates dramatically on an east-west axis. Its flow is interrupted by a central, triangular wing which contains the dining rooms. Mitchell and Giurgola of Philadelphia were chosen as the architects. Their prior work had shown an imaginative play of forms and interesting structural techniques.

The building was originally designed to house four separate dining rooms. This proved to be way over budget so eventually there was only one large dining hall in the central mass, which juts out to the south. The room is all glass on its south side and has wonderful views up the hill towards Chapin and Williams Hall. The spirit of the building is somewhat different than Greylock, which is more geometric, more rectangular, blockier. Mission Park has curving forms with cylindrical

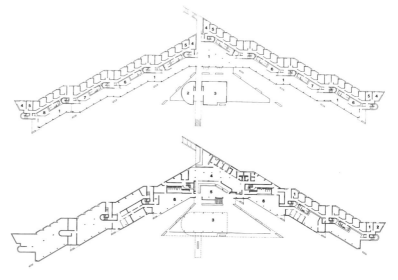

TOP
Construction from north with Thompson Infirmary in lower right (WHT, 1971)

RIGHT
First-floor plan:
    1 main corridor
    2, 3 meeting rooms

BOTTOM RIGHT
Ground-floor plan, dining room in lower center

South façade
from the west

East and north
façades

"The most photogenic
Williams building"

stairwells that play against flat surfaces which remind one somewhat of the work of Le Corbusier. The southern mass has a fascinating jagged surface with a series of curves that frame the dining room's acute angles. Views on page 133 from the south show this dynamically treated wall. A detail, taken just around the corner, shows a stairwell played against part of the north face.

The building was built of reinforced concrete and the exterior sheathed in prefabricated concrete panels shipped down from Canada. Of interest is a continuous corridor along the south side of the building on the main floor. The three bedroom floors above are grouped in series of four or five oddly shaped bedrooms and a bath. The corridor idea had been used very successfully in a big dormitory in a Scottish college by James Stirling, the English architect, whereas the undulating wall with the geometric dining room has a connection with Alvar Aalto's Baker Hall at MIT.

This is quite a different concept from the multiple buildings of Greylock. It is a totally different approach to the housing and feeding of students.

*Student room
(Ronnie Freer,
c. 1972)*

Interior of dining room, from the west.

First-floor hall

The Amos Lawrence Hopkins Memorial Forest

1971

The Hopkins Memorial Forest is a 2,500-acre tract a mile and a half northwest of the campus. A century ago the land was largely the farm (Buxton Farms) of Amos Lawrence Hopkins, the sixth of ten children of Mary Hubble and Mark Hopkins, then President of the College. The only remaining farm building is the carriage house and horse stable, constructed in 1906, complete with a tower clock that strikes the hour.

After Hopkins died in 1912 his wife continued the farm for another dozen years before auctioning off most of the equipment and disposing of the livestock. In November 1933, Mrs. Hopkins gave the Buxton Farms to the College as a memorial to her late husband and the trustees worked with the U.S. Forest Service to establish the Hopkins Memorial Forest as a research facility.

Between 1935 and 1968 the Forest Service conducted research on hydrology, forest growth and tree genetics in the Hopkins Forest. Officials converted the second story of the carriage house to be a dorm for 45 Civilian Conservation Corps men, who worked at the Forest in the mid-1930s. Later the building became a combined residence and a depot for trucks.

In April 1968, the USFS returned the Hopkins Memorial Forest to Williams and vacated the site.

The College decided in 1971 that a Center for Environmental Studies should use the site for environmental education and research. Students took advantage of the recreational opportu-

1906 Carriage Barn (HWA)

nities of the newly accessible trails and registered for independent study opportunities and summer research positions. The permanent forest inventory plots established by the USFS in the 1930s were reinventoried to determine changes that had occurred over the 35-year period.

Peter B. McChesney '75 wrote a proposal for the establishment of the Hopkins Forest Farm Museum which is housed in a barn from the Moon family farm, located in the center of Buxton Farms. The moving and renovation of the Moon Barn was completed in 1976.

In 1977, a grant from the National Science Foundation allowed the renovation of the carriage barn into a field lab, classroom and office complex and caretaker's residence. In October 1979 the

renovated carriage barn was officially dedicated as the Rosenburg Center in honor of Arthur E. and Ella M. Rosenburg, caretakers of the property for many years.

Hopkins Forest is used for many courses in Environmental Studies, Biology, Geosciences, and even Studio Art and Religion. Long-term research of the changes in the landscape over time and the role of human history and its influences on biological and geological processes are studied. In addition, the College has initiated limited experimental studies requiring the manipulation of small areas of forest.

(Submitted by Henry W. Art, director of the Center for Environmental Studies and former director of the Hopkins Memorial Forest.)

Mather House
(Admissions Office)

1971

Mather House was built on the corner of Park and Main Streets where the Faculty Club is now located, sometime in the late 1830s. A building of straightforward timber construction, it was the home of the Benjamin Mather family and also housed their general store. It remained a store until the College bought it in 1951 and moved it to its present location to house the Honors program, the office of Phi Beta Kappa and a faculty apartment. Thus it remained until 1971 when it became the Admissions building. If vibes could come out of walls, pre-frosh would be bathed in the art of shopkeeping and the art of being very bright and working hard to become Phi Beta Kappa. They would have a good thrust into a prosperous future.

This is a very simple building and seems to me a very fine home for Admissions. It's been added to and added to, but admissions still needs a lot more room. Plans for future construction indicate that the building will be moved again, but that's not new to Williamstown houses. They've all been moved at least once.

The interior of Mather retains its residential small scale and projects a nice domestic atmosphere. It is furnished with a great many antiques which were a gift of an alumnus some years ago.

TOP
From Main Street

ABOVE
Reception area

137

Women's Athletic Facility

Lockwood Greene, 1971

With the arrival of the first women undergraduates in 1969 and the first entering class including women in 1971, the College needed women's shower and locker rooms in the gym. Through a stroke of luck there was an empty space between the expanded Lasell Gym of 1928 and the squash courts of 1938, above a basement-level passageway that connected the main gym with the squash building. This void was filled, quite economically as it turned out, with locker rooms for women with easy access to all of the college's athletic facilities. There was even room for a dance studio on the top floor.

Between Lasell and the Squash Building

"Inexpensive; a roof and two side walls"

Tyler Annex

Unitec Inc./Lindstrom and Associates, 1972

An interesting technique to increase student housing was to add to former fraternity houses. The old Psi Upsilon house off Park Street is one example. Now called Tyler, the building has an addition to the east curving along the driveway and providing dramatic views of Pine Cobble. The addition is very sympathetic to the architecture of the fraternity. It is brick and quite sculptural on both sides, nicely related to the old building. Residents here eat just down the hill at Mission Park.

ABOVE RIGHT
*Under construction
(WHT, 1972)*

RIGHT
From the southwest

"New blended in well with old"

Dodd House

1974

The original section of Dodd House was built in 1880 by Cyrus Morris Dodd, class of 1855 and professor of mathematics at Williams from 1869 until his death in 1897. That part of the building seems, from early photographs, to be of eclectic Swiss chalet style.

Upon professor Dodd's death, his daughters, Grace and Alice, operated a boarding house called Netherleigh in the residence, adding a wing to the north in 1902. In 1909 the building was purchased by a group of Williams alumni in order to provide accomodations for visitors close to campus. They named it the Williams Alumni House.

The house was enlarged by additions to the south for a lounge and rooms above, and the dining room and kitchen were extended to the north. In 1913 the name was changed to The Williams Inn and leased to the Treadway Inns group. In 1956 the corporation known as the Williams Alumni House, Inc., was dissolved and the building became the property of the president and trustees of Williams College. The building was leased to the Treadways until a new Inn was completed in 1974, at which time the building was renamed Dodd House and converted for use as a dormitory and dining room. The building's warmth and charm, and private bathrooms, make it a favorite with today's students.

Dodd in center background with auxiliary buildings on left and right, from the west.

The original Dodd House (anon., 1897)

"The students like the old hotel johns"

*Student residents
of Dodd House
at the west entrance
(Multipics, 1978)*

Sawyer Library

Harry Weese and Associates, 1976

TOP
From the southeast

ABOVE
Construction, from the east (WHT, 1974)

OPPOSITE
Inside the east attrium

Determining the location of the Sawyer Library was complicated by a lack of space in the center of the campus. An aerial photograph of the construction shows the new library and its relationship to the old library – Stetson – and the nearby Chapin and Baxter halls. Sawyer, a rectangular box squeezed into the middle of the campus, required the demolition of the former Sigma Phi fraternity house. This was a reconstruction of the Van Rensselaer Manor, an 18th-century house in Albany, N.Y., modified by James Renwick in the mid-19th-century, and brought to the campus and redesigned by Marcus Reynolds, class of 1890.

Sawyer is central to the campus and its plan creates a flow of traffic through and around it with entries from the east and the west through courtyards. Sawyer has basement, mezzanine and

three main floors. The exterior is overly simple. There is a brick arcade along the south side of the building containing low windows that illuminate the basement. The arcade dominates the south façade of the building. The east and west entrances are at the base of gradual ramps and open onto a lobby which has stairs which lead up one flight to the main floor. Atria above the ramps are open to the sky to provide natural lighting in surrounding study carrels on the top two floors. Bridges on those two floors create the fourth side of the atria. The main circulation desk is at the top of the stairs from the entry lobby. Computers, which have replaced card catalogues, are everywhere on that first floor which also contains the reference materials and staff offices.

From the point of view of a library, the upper two floors are the most interesting because it is here that the architects have tried to accommodate all different ways to study. During the design process they built several varieties of study carrels in the old library and got reactions from students. As a result, the new building contains relatively "normal" desk and study-table areas – as well as structures you can crawl into, climb up onto, or sit at and enjoy a variety of views. A great deal of time was spent trying to find out what students wanted. The study-area aspect of the Sawyer library seems to me to be very successful visually, and it certainly has proven to be successful functionally as well. It is extremely popular with students and work stations are at a premium, especially in the days leading up to exam periods.

Third floor plan

*Study areas
looking north*

Bernhard Music Center

Cambridge Seven, 1979

Until Bernhard was constructed, the music department had been jammed into Currier Hall, in space converted from a dining room and student living quarters. It now would have a wonderful home of its own. The architectural firm of Cambridge Seven was hired and its lead architect, John Jordan, and his associate, Terry Rankine, headed the project.

This building's architectural and functional attachments to Chapin have proven very successful. Chapin, an isolated building, had been under-utilized. It was used occasionally for concerts, lectures and sometimes formal academic ceremonies. This music center plan involved remodeling the basement of Chapin, installing practice rooms, a lounge and kitchenette and storage rooms for instruments. All that had to be done to get room for this was to move President Phinney Baxter's archives out of basement store rooms.

The architects were particularly sensitive to setting a building next to Chapin, making it lower so as not to detract from the impact of the big scale of the Chapin façade. The addition is sort of driven into the side of Chapin so that it looks as though it has always been there. The choice of a building material was complicated by the varieties of brick used in the three surrounding buildings – Sawyer, Lehman and Chapin. So, the architects used concrete, putting horizontal indentations in the surface which relate to the corner treatment of Chapin. It is possible, though I think highly accidental, that these horizontal markings are suggestive of a music staff.

The bottom floor of the building has offices for the Music Department and

"A gem of a building, linked successfully to Chapin"

TOP
Architects' rendering

ABOVE
From the east (WHT, 1978)

OPPOSITE
Lobby outside Brooks-Rogers Recital Hall, showing entrance to Chapin

classrooms. Upstairs the main foyer has a
very dramatic cantilever and offers direct
access into Brooks-Rogers, a fine lecture
and music hall. Its design allows for music
classes as well as the heavily enrolled
introductory art history course. This is a
multifaceted room that gets a tremendous
amount of use and I think it is well
designed. Also on this floor are a choral
room and an orchestral rehearsal room.

The space between Chapin and the
Music Center is interesting because it
holds a series of sculptures by H. Lee
Hirsche who ran the studio art program for years. These are made to look
as if they are constructed from parts
of musical instruments and they are
placed underneath roof drains so water
runs onto them when it rains, creating
intriguing fluid patterns and "running
water" sounds. In the winter, the freez-
ing water creates fascinating ice forms.

A comment about how Williams selects
its architects: in the early days of the
College, architects had been selected by
the President and the Trustees. Starting
in the early 1960s, with the planning
of the Greylock complex, students
became somewhat involved, working
with the selected architects. Beginning
with the construction of Bernhard, a
committee composed mostly of members of the Music Department, with an
administrator and students, screened
architects, visiting them and their
previous work. Their top choices were
submitted to the President and the
Trustees for a final selection. This procedure was inaugurated by President
John Chandler and has continued to be
followed. I would argue that it might
be a good idea to have an architectural
historian from the Art Department
added to these committees.

Brooks-Rogers
Recital Hall

OPPOSITE
Lee Hirsche's
sculpture court

Williams College Museum of Art

Phase 1: Moore, Grover and Harper, 1983

Phase 2: Centerbrook Architects and Planners, 1986

Although these two phases of the addition to the College museum were done at slightly different dates it seems more sensible to talk about the building as a whole. The view from the north shows what the building looked like when the addition and the renovation took place.

The central core of the building is the octagon of 1847 (Lawrence Hall). In 1890, wings had been added to the east and the west. In 1926-7, a large wing on the south side was extended east-west to contain the Lawrence Art Museum on the top floor and the Classics Department on the ground floor. The museum had only a large lecture room and one small gallery in addition, of course, to the galleries in the octagon and its adjoining wings. In 1938, an addition, the Blashfield Wing, had filled the void between the west wing and the big lecture hall.

For the new additions, Charles Moore, whom we had known before as he had assisted Lee Hirsche in teaching archi-tecture, was the architect. He is one of the most famous of the post-modern architects. The first phase was a whole new building to the south of Lawrence. The site was a flat area that dropped off steeply to the south. The wing that was put on had a big atrium that became the connecting link between the old and the new sections. The building that steps down the slope has, on its top floor, one very large gallery (the 1954 Gallery) and a smaller one. Besides the atrium, the ground floor

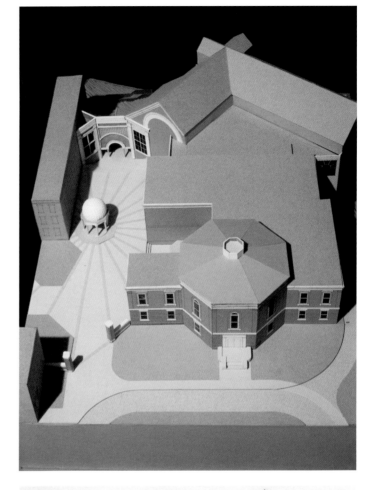

Architects' model, first stage (Moore, 1980)

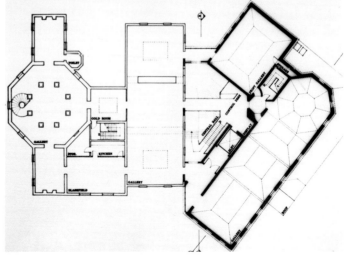

Top-floor plan (Moore, 1980)

ABOVE
From the north

FAR LEFT
The south wall from the west

LEFT
The "ironic" columns

contains museum storage, the print room and a small gallery. The next level down includes a lecture hall and Art Department slide room and offices. The bottom floor contains rooms which were meant for studio space but became additional storage for the museum. This first phase added a tremendous amount of teaching space, and long-awaited room for the slide room and offices.

In the second phase, as seen from the northeast, there are a west wing and an infill which contains galleries at two levels. Renovations refurbished old rooms, adding fireproofing, a major contribution to the safety of the building. On the south side the building has four levels. At the lowest level is a back entrance with Ironic Order columns, a Charles Moore invention. His idea of cantilevering the space (used for a faculty lounge and offices) gives the back of the building an interesting composition. He called these spaces "saddlebags."

ABOVE RIGHT
The opening (JMK, 1986)

RIGHT
The atrium, looking east

The '54 gallery at the opening of the Moore show (WCMA, 1986)

The atrium, looking west

Going into the building from the east, one finds the atrium both surprising and exciting. It is entirely involved with the juncture of old and new. Spaces are animated. Stairways leave going both up and down. Three bridges connect different parts of the building. Moore repeats some of the classical details from the Greek Revival octagon at the ends of the middle bridge. You have the feeling that you're walking around in the middle of a Piranesi print of the *Carceri* (Prisons). The big gallery that goes along the south side is very large with high ceilings. (It is illustrated here holding the Moore retrospective exhibition that opened the building.) The rest of the galleries in the building are much smaller and all different.

This is, I think, a very special building. To my mind the atrium is the most interesting interior space on the Williams campus. In 1992, a few years after designing this complex, Charles Moore won the Gold Medal of the American Institute of Architects.

ABOVE RIGHT
The exterior of the new '35 Gallery

RIGHT
The rotunda, with sculpture by Morris. This area originally housed the college library. (JMK, 1986)

OPPOSITE
The '35 Gallery

Faculty Club Addition

Cambridge Seven, 1983

This relatively large addition strengthened and markedly improved the functioning of the Faculty Club. The addition is a two-story mass to the west that has a dining room on the top floor and an informal room, with a bar, on the bottom floor. The corner of the addition and the old building creates two sides of a rather extensive patio for informal eating. Glass doors open from both the dining room and from the connecting hallway, providing access to this terrace.

The addition has a pedimented roof running north-south that echoes the pedimented west and south sides of the old building. The new dining room has a strip fenestration around the top, a direct attempt to make the new construction appear to be an intricate part of the old structure.

All in all, this is a fine addition to the Alumni Center/Faculty House.

TOP
The addition from the south

ABOVE
New dining room

AMT Addition: Theater-in-the-Round

Cambridge Seven, 1983

This addition both permitted the expansion of the variety of productions the College could put on, and made the AMT accessible to handicapped by providing a new way to get into the AMT main stage area.

The new auditorium is nearly a theater-in-the-round with seats in an arc around three sides of the stage. The exterior is a rectangular mass in the re-entrant angle of the old AMT auditorium and its workshop wing. The surface is animated with relieving arches into which windows have been set.

There is nothing terribly fascinating about this, but it is a good example of perfectly straightforward designing.

TOP
The addition from the west

ABOVE
The Merchant of Venice (CC, 1986)

Jesup Computer Center

John Jordan, 1984

"Nothing can hurt this already crippled building"

As if Jesup had not suffered through the ages with having practically everybody use it for their home base for years, the final blow was the occupation by the computers.

The whole building was gutted, losing a wonderful theater and lecture hall. Each floor is now filled with offices or computer labs. The teaching of computer sciences is being done in the new Unified Science Center.

To make the conversion of Jesup possible, and to modernize it, access towers had to be put on both ends. On the north the tower is set back slightly from the face of the building and on the south the tower is recessed further and goes up a little bit higher. These towers have staircases and elevators. I haven't the remotest idea what goes on in the building, but I assume that everybody there knows exactly what they're doing.

From the northwest

Mary Clark Thompson Center for Health Services

David J. Westall, 1985

The Thompson Health Services building at the bottom of Hoxsey Street is set in the woods. It is a one-story brick structure, L-shaped. At the corner is a pedimented entrance with classical motifs. The most interesting thing about the building is the way the brick was used to create interesting patterns.

From the northeast

Faculty Art Studio
Burr and McCallum, 1985

This small structure houses four studios for the studio art faculty. It's nestled down under Driscoll Dining Hall and up against the old heating plant that itself once provided space for teaching studio art. It is a very simple structure with a corrugated metal exterior. Light is admitted through a north clerestory on a raised section of the roof. This is a very straightforward design using modern materials.

From the west

"Handsome and hidden"

From the east

Chandler Athletic Facility
Cambridge Seven Associates, 1987

The basic hurdle that had to be jumped to build this building was to get it into an area bounded on the southeast by the hockey rink and on the west by the back of the stores on Spring Street. It needed to be there to be convenient to the town and the students and to utilize the refurbished old Lasell facilities.

The College needed an Olympic-length, eight-lane pool with a diving area, which could also be used for water polo, as well as a basketball court with adequate spectator accommodations. Shoehorning the resulting two masses and their adjacent circulation areas into the available space was quite an accomplishment.

The pool runs north/south, parallel to the hockey rink. It contains two moveable bulkheads that permit diving, racing and warming up in their own sections of the main area. Spectators for swim meets have a large elevated gallery along the west wall. The pool meets not only the College's aquatic needs but is available to and used by the Williamstown community and area high schools and youth organizations.

The basketball area contains a central intercollegiate court with retractable bleachers, all running east/west. With the bleachers rolled back, the space can be split east/west, using curtains, to provide individual team practice, physical education or intramural accommodations. The floor is also used by the volleyball teams and the room provides an ideal space for such large functions as the annual meeting of the Society of Alumni and academic ceremonies.

The east façade, looking past the Hockey Rink

Spring Street storefronts in the Chandler building

OPPOSITE RIGHT
Architect's Model

OPPOSITE FAR RIGHT
Ground floor plan

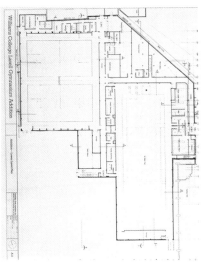

The new building is connected to the squash courts, and through them to the Lasell gym, by a second story enclosed hallway running as a bridge over the north side arcade. The bridge contains a photo display honoring retired Williams coaches.

The Spring Street façade has three store fronts that reflect other simple brick structures seen all up and down the east side of the street. On the north side of the stores a passage leads underneath the bridge to a large courtyard formed by the gym, the art museum and the Simon Squash Courts, as well as to the entrance to Chandler.

This project included major renovations inside the Lasell building, including reconstruction of the locker and showers rooms, to provide for a larger and coeducational student body, and the conversion of the old swimming pool to a two story area. On the bottom floor, actually in the old pool, rowing tanks were installed for the crews to use for practice. On an upper floor, at the level of the top of the old pool spectator area, a weight and exercise room was created.

The architecture of the gym, as viewed from the courtyard, is not overly exciting. The fun side of the courtyard is created by the south wall of the art museum. The courtyard needs to be more active. Perhaps a central sculpture piece (the result of a student competition?) could invigorate this attractive location.

The exercise room

OPPOSITE TOP
Pick-up basketball game

OPPOSITE BOTTOM
The Muir-Samuelson pool

Weston Field and Plansky Track

Saratoga Associates, 1987

Improvements to the athletic fields on Weston Field concluded a chapter in the development of athletic facilities on the campus. A new baseball diamond, named for long-time baseball coach Bobby Coombs and a new track, converted to Olympic size and named for veteran track coach Tony Plansky, joined a relocated football field. New aluminum stands (cold on your rear) and a new and larger press box/equipment building combine to make the whole area functional and good looking. The College often makes this field available for nearby high schools to use in dual and regional competitions.

Football field, from the south, with relocated 1890's Peck Grandstand on the left (west side of the field)

OPPOSITE
Weston Field, the Williams/Amherst game (DB, 1997)

Hopkins Hall Addition

Architectural Resources, 1989

It is difficult to put an addition on a building as unique as Hopkins Hall. With an almost square plan, Hopkins was built using lots of materials of different colors, making it nearly impossible to copy. On the other hand, a glass box stuck on the back of it would have been out of keeping with the campus as a whole. A compromise had to be made and this group of architects was quite successful in creating an obviously new addition which utilizes some of the feature of the old building and is therefore sympathetic to the original.

The architects simplified the materials problems by sticking to one color of brick, but retaining the relatively long and thin shape of the bricks used in the old building. They also picked up the pedimented gables that ran along the superstructure of Hopkins. The theme of these is repeated in more staccato terms with steeper ones and more of them on the addition. There is no stone in the addition (as there is in the original) but the form of the windows is generally carred through, so there is a marriage, but still a separation, between the old and the new.

Inside, problems were caused by the high ceilings in the old building and the levels of the windows. Matching new floors to old window heights required some ingenuity. The building was gutted, the basement floor lowered, and a whole new, extended interior was built with five floors replacing what had been a four-story plus basement interior.

The interior spaces work very well, although the halls seem a little over designed and certainly over lit. There are Socratic-style classrooms on the

lowest level and regular classrooms on the top three stories (there are none on the "first" floor). The classrooms are interspersed among administrative offices creating interesting traffic patterns. A handsome seminar room on the top floor offers spectacular views in all directions.

The north façade is very fancy and it seem to me it is screaming to be used as the backdrop of an opera, something like *Aida*, because there is certainly room for the elephants.

*"Screaming to be
used as the back-
drop of an opera"*

The Oakley Center

1989

In 1983/84, a small group of interested faculty met to discuss the possibility of developing a humanities center at Williams College to support multidisciplinary faculty research. President John Chandler appointed a committee of faculty from a number of different disciplines to study the feasibility of such a center and in the fall of 1985 the College established the Center for the Humanities and Social Sciences. The Center's primary goal was to encourage sustained intellectual exchanges among faculty members whose scholarship and teaching bridge traditional disciplinary boundaries. By bringing together scholars from different fields, the College hoped to create an opportunity for collaborative discussions about fundamental questions of human society and thought as they manifest themselves in literature, the arts, and social and political institutions.

At the 1989 Convocation, the College celebrated the official opening of the Center's permanent home in Makepeace House on the edge of the campus. This lovely old New England home provides offices for Fellows who remain in residence for either one or two semesters. Typically, fellows are usually Williams faculty on leave but occasionally faculty from other institutions enjoy visiting appointments to the Center. Each semester Fellows present their ongoing work at a weekly seminar. Additional Center programs, designed to enrich the intellectual life on campus, include semester long seminars and discussion groups organized by Williams faculty, conferences on selected topics, and colloquia and symposia by distinguished scholars who come to campus for brief residencies.

Dining/lecture room

Many of these latter events are open to the public and to nearby colleges and universities.

In 1993, in recognition of his many contributions to Williams College, including his founding role in establishing the Center, the Board of Trustees honored President Francis Oakley by renaming 70 Center the Oakley Center for the Humanities and Social Sciences. Today the Oakley Center continues to be a vital resource in the intellectual life of the College. It is a place where faculty from different disciplines can work together and explore new areas of inquiry and a forum for community-wide discussion of important issues relevant to current scholarly debates.

Submitted by Robert D. Kavanaugh, director of the Oakley Center

Makepeace House,
east façade

Jewish Religious Center

Herbert Newman Associates, 1990

This Religious Center has a tightly organized and fascinating plan offering lots of flexibility. The largest room, the bima, under the skylight and the projecting roof, is where religious services take place. It is basically an octagonal shape and has three interior walls on the east that disappear up into the ceiling so that the space can be opened up for larger affairs, such as weddings or lectures. The north end of the building, towards Main Street, has kitchens and a meeting room. The south side holds a large living room that wraps around the religious center. This is a plan with spaces that can be expanded or contracted depending upon how you arrange the moveable walls.

This complexity of function means that the massing of the exterior is somewhat complicated, but I think the masses play against each other quite nicely. The building is located just south of Weston Language Lab, and it is surrounded, perhaps overly so, by trees.

The bima

West façade

From the northwest

"Fascinating and flexible"

Stetson Apartments Renovation

Einhorn, Yaffee, Prescott, 1993

As the College's needs changed, the Stetson Apartments (Poker Flats) were converted from faculty housing to student housing. It's rather ironic that quite a bit of money was spent making the apartments nicer for students than they ever had been for faculty. Extensions were added on both the south and the north sides to get porches and extra rooms for each unit. These are co-op housing for upper classmen doing their own housekeeping. These additions transform one dull long rectangle into three different masses that are much more interesting. It's not only better looking; it's also much nicer inside.

Entrance porches, from the southwest

> *"Better living now that it is for students"*

CES Matt Cole Library
(addition to Kellogg House)
Ann Beha Associates (Pamela Hawkes '75), 1995

The Williams College Environmental-Studies Program started in 1967 and spent several years in various buildings before finally moving into the Kellogg House. Kellogg was built on the site now occupied by Hopkins Hall in the 1790's. It was first moved north to the future site of Stetson and when Stetson was built, in 1922, was moved further north, down the hill to its present location. George Washington didn't sleep here, but Mark Hopkins did.

There have been two additions to the building, both to house the large environmental library, a unique aspect of the Williams program. The first addition was to the south and the second, a much larger structure, was added to the northwest corner. This is a series of interestingly arranged spaces and the exterior blends nicely with the old house. The south addition now contains the program's offices.

Kellogg, which had housed faculty until it was converted for the Environmental Center, is a nice 18th-century building.

ABOVE RIGHT
From the north-east, library on right

RIGHT
From the west, Kellogg's east façade

"An unusually tasteful, modern addition"

Chaffee Tennis House and Hunt '44 Tennis Center

Chris Williams, 1993

At the southwest corner of the College tennis courts, on the corner of Stetson Road and Lynde Lane, is the Clarence Chaffee Tennis House, which, together with six new hard courts, forms the core of the Torrance M. Hunt '44 Tennis Center. The building was designed by College architect Chris Williams and is a simple structure that straddles the right angle made by the two streets. It has a spectacular deck overlooking the tennis courts and providing a grand view of Pine Cobble.

The left hand mass has a room containing trophies and memorabilia of Chaffee's extraordinary 32-year career as the coach of the College's tennis, squash and soccer teams. The right hand mass contains men's and women's bathroom facilities. There is a ground floor room with an entrance underneath the spectator deck which provides space for the storage of equipment.

Spectator deck, from the south

OPPOSITE TOP
From the southwest

OPPOSITE BOTTOM
Tournament courts, spectactor deck and house from the east bleachers

Spencer Studio Art Building

Carlos Jiminez/Cambridge Seven, 1996

At long last Williams College has a studio building and it's a wonderful one. The studio people had suffered long enough in the cellar of the Greylock dining hall with no windows, in parts of the ex-Rudnick Laundry, in portions of the former Steele & Cleary garage and then Goodrich, but a Goodrich which had to be shared with other disciplines.

Finally, the College got a wonderful new building by a Costa Rican architect whom the studio people discovered in Texas through a publication of his work. He excels in natural lighting and has a real flair for making a building sympathetic to its specific environment.

Viewing the building from the north, one can see in the left-hand mass where the painting studio is located on the top floor with its high ceilings. The print-makers with their presses and studio carrels are one floor down. To the far left of this mass is the sculpture section. The unusual feature of this main mass is a big cantilever out over the entranceway that has offices above it and the staircase and all circulation inside it. That circulation is expressed by a vertical tier of windows, and that tier plays off against the horizontal windows of the chairman's office, which is inside the cantilever itself.

The subtlety of this exterior rests in the role of the four brick pilasters which pick up the pilasters in an adjacent addition to the Methodist Church. The architect has unified the buildings and the space defined by the art building, the Church addition, and the Williamstown Savings Bank.

Sculpture studio

The interiors have wide halls which everyone originally thought were very lavish but they are places for studio work to be hung, a continuous gallery that is filled with student work. The wing that goes north to south contains rooms for architecture, basic design and video. Williams now has a video artist on its staff. Sculpture has a whole wing overlooking the Williamstown fire station and has high overhead doors that open onto an enclosed garden south of the building. The site is elevated so the building has marvelous views of the mountains. It's a straight modern building that I think has little touches reminiscent of Le Corbusier but it's basically Jiminez, a very good architect who has done many lovely buildings in Texas.

The building has two features that I think are important. Besides having offices for all the studio art staff there is

a small gallery on the main floor that changes exhibits twice a month using student work. Above it is a classroom that has all the equipment for showing prints and slides. This is a teaching building and I think it is extremely successful. Although it is at the extreme eastern end of the campus it is only a short way from the Williams College Museum of Art.

From the southeast

From the northwest

*"A splendid eastern
campus boundry
with great views"*

Goodrich Hall Renovation

Bruner/Cott Associates, 1998

It was a very important campus event when the Goodrich Chapel/Alumni Hall building was miraculously converted from a church that had been in turn a mix of art studios and lecture rooms, with a second floor run through the main sanctuary, into a student-run cafe with a bar serving all kinds of coffee, cocoa, donuts, etc. In fact, the coffee bar is located in what was once the transept of Goodrich which had been added onto the original building. The whole notion of this new plan was to have a place run by students for students, containing a room in which each student organization had its own secured desk and files. The need for this sort of space was great because Baxter was just not big enough and Jesup could no longer be carved up by everybody because it now housed computers.

The former nave of the chapel now has two aisles holding a gallery. Steel was used here so the new construction wouldn't detract from the original wooden structure. The whole interior becomes a wonderful space with people studying in the gallery, getting together in meeting rooms or just talking and drinking coffee in the main "church" room. The stage is outfitted with all kinds of lighting and acoustical appliances so you can have any kind of function you want there.

The "great room" has a high wooden ceiling that comes to a peak in a typical Gothic vein with the stage at the south end. Beyond it are the rooms used by the various organizations, bathrooms and an elevator. With activities ranging from skits to *a capella* singing to lectures. this is a fun place and it functions well.

The old 1859 chapel and alumni building has taken on an entirely new life that is an active and positive one. And besides, how many cafés have their own stained glass window?

ABOVE
Nave, looking north (WSS, 1999)

RIGHT
Café in the west transept (WSS, 1999)

From the north

**"Dramatic new life
for an old Gothic
chapel"**

179

Simon Squash Courts

Michael Wurmfeld, 1998

"A very creative and active addition"

In the 1990s, the U.S. squash organizations decided that the game of squash would be improved considerably by increasing the width of the regulation squash court to standardize our dimensions with the rest of the world. Since Williams plays intercollegiate squash with everybody, including many Division I teams, it was necessary to build new courts, as other schools were doing. A problem arose when it was discovered that the walls of the existing squash courts were bearing walls, holding up the floor above. They couldn't just be moved laterally. That meant an enormously costly operation of gutting the structure and building a new interior, putting an addition to the east towards the Williams College Art Museum.

It is of interest to note that if the Museum, several years before, hadn't reduced the length of its big gallery to bring price into line with budget, there wouldn't have been room for this eastern expansion of the squash courts. This addition considerably enlarged the original squash extension. It contains a lovely outside entrance and lounge area on a diagonal in the northwest corner of the courtyard that is surrounded by the Museum, the gym and the pool.

The entrance way is very handsomely designed and is adjacent to a staircase that connects the courtyard with the upper level of the campus and more specifically, Goodrich Hall. A second staircase leads to the Museum and in between them is a small garden with a piece of sculpture by Herbert Ferber.

The addition contains a dozen new squash courts, nine of which have glass back walls, providing, for the first time,

excellent accommodation for spectators at Williams squash matches. While the old courts had hardwood walls, the new ones are of special plaster that was imported from England, along with the crew that applied the material. The courts have hardwood floors that are floated on a sponge-like base that allows them to give when you walk on them.

The interior spaces include a two-story lounge/main entrance lobby overlooked by offices for the squash coaches. A third-floor area, behind the upper level courts, houses exercise equipment. This is a very popular space with students, faculty and staff.

The Spring Street façade of the squash building didn't change much although new landscaping in front created an attractive park-like area with benches which attract both students and Spring Street shoppers.

TOP
Entrance on the plaza, from the southeast.

ABOVE
Court number one

OPPOSITE
Lobby with Coach Dave Johnson on balcony at upper left talking to Williams Squash All-American Zafrir Levy '01.

The Morley Unified Science Center
Zimmer Gunsul Frasca, and Einhorn Yaffee Prescott, 2000

The Science Center is the largest and most complex architectural enterprise in Williams history. Its construction was complicated by the need to continue teaching the sciences while the new facility was built and old ones were renovated. The number of different departments and the need to shuffle the spaces they occupied during the construction process dictated extremely careful planning.

The building is named after Professor Edward Morley, class of 1860 and a member of the science faculty of Western Reserve College in Ohio for 14 years after the Civil War. Besides teaching courses in most of the sciences and in mathematics, he did world renowned research to determine the relative masses of oxygen and hydrogen atoms. His later research on the movement of the earth, the Michelson-Morley experiments, using apparatus the two men developed themselves, laid the groundwork for Einstein's Theory of Relativity. Morley died in 1923, leaving what remained of his equipment and a large bequest to Williams.

Development of the Morley Science Center started in 1992 when the president and trustees voted to modernize the chemistry building with new labs and office spaces, and to construct a building which would be a science library, bringing all of the science research materials into one place for the first time. Before this each science had its own library within the confines of the discipline and all of them had outgrown their allocated spaces.

Professor Charles Lovett, chairman of the chemistry department and director

of the Bronfman Science Center, was put in charge of the project. Soon it became apparent that all of the sciences were in dire need of additional space and a general upgrading of their teaching areas, as nothing had really been done in this area since the construction of Bronfman in 1967.

The committee planning the new facilities visited other campuses and quickly determined that one building housing all of the sciences best fit the needs of Williams. An architectural planning firm was retained to research the space required to house the programs that the faculties envisioned, and to select a location (behind the three Thompson Science Labs, linking them with Bronfman). The president and trustees approved the plan and a $40 million budget in early 1994.

The next job for the committee was screening architects and after visiting buildings done by several, recommended a half dozen for on-campus interviews. The committee finally backed the firm of Zimmer, Gunsel, Frasca, recipient of an AIA Architectural Firm Award in 1991. They were chosen primarily because of their ability to preserve existing buildings and to integrate them into new construction – just what was needed for the Morley project.

The interdisciplinary uses of Bronfman were retained while the new construction was given over to the creation of modern lab facilities for the individual departments. Old labs in the Thompson buildings were converted to additional offices, classrooms and auditorium spaces.

"Fascinating solutions to a myriad of problems"

Study areas are scat-
tered throughout the
building. This one, at
the east end of the the
third floor hallway,
offers a spectacular
view across Spring
Street to the mountains

RIGHT
Lobby inside
the north
entrance

The library for the combined sciences, the need for which was the primary motivation for the project, occupies the whole area south of the old Thompson Science buildings. Some small additions behind, to the south of, the Thompson buildings were demolished to open up this area for the new construction. The entire bottom floor, opening on ground level to the south, one story below the first floor as one enters from the science quad, is given over to the stacks, read-ing/study areas and circulation desk of the science library.

The two spaces between the three Thompson buildings were roofed over, enclosed but left open. Their concrete and glass ceilings and walls provide nat-ural light for the library and for the sur-rounding classrooms, labs and offices which have windows opening into them.

The interior walls of the atria consist either of the brick exterior walls of the

old Thompson buildings or of new construction – walls of concrete painted in subtle pastels or incorporat-ing large expanses of glass. The result-ing spaces are wonderful.

The Science quad entrance to the com-plex is through a three-story, convex glass wall that connects Physics and Chemistry. The foyer which this creates leads up to an east/west passage that provides access to corridors which tie the buildings together and also down to the main library entrance. In the foyer, as in other spaces, the original brickwork and the stone footings are left exposed and contrast subtly with the new construction.

Since the Thompson labs, for some strange reason, were constructed at dif-ferent levels, there was a problem when the three buildings were joined. Ramps were needed to complete the union and this created some odd-shaped spaces.

*East atrium contains
the library's circula-
tion desk and
reference and
periodical areas*

*Students at work
in an MSC lab*

*West atrium holds
library stacks, a
reading area and
individual study
carrels*

These have been furnished and seem to be appreciated by students as they are in constant use as reading, study or conversation areas.

The main Morley entrance is on the east facade, behind the old Physics building and it has an interesting post-modern portico that gives into a lobby housing a museum dedicated to Professor Morley's career and achievements.

Above the portico is a large glass-walled section which allows light to flood into seating areas at the ends of the east/west corridors on both upper floors. These offer spectacular views

over the town to the mountains.

A fringe benefit of the construction was the creation of new access routes to the campus. A pedestrian way to Spring Street is provided by a stairway leading to Bank Street. Vehicular access from the south comes off of Mecham Street and leads to both a traffic circle near the east entrance and to a loading dock on the west end of the addition.

The Morley Science Center was completed in December of 2000, eight years after it was conceived. Not only the newest building on campus, it represents the epitome to date of the

logical planning of architectural development on the Williams campus. This is demonstrated by the extensive use of the committee process, involving the eventual users, in selecting the architects and contractors who created the building.

It is fitting that the building is named for a scientist whose own life and career were as multi-disciplinary as is the Center. With 40 percent of Williams students taking science courses, it is certain that the building will be well utilized. In fact, with it, Williams is poised to move into the future of science.

Appendices

OPPOSITE
*The Williams Club
New York City*

Buildings Gone but not Forgotten

By Sylvia Kennick Brown and Linda Hall

Photos from WCA

See illustration in main text, p. 21

See illustration in main text, p. 33

East College (Old), 1798

The original East College was so named because of its placement on the "eastern eminence" of the village in 1798. Funds for the much-needed building came from the sale of two Maine townships granted to the college by the Massachusetts legislature. The four story, 104 by 28-foot, brick building was similar to West College but had two halls going through it east to west instead of one, and there were two bedrooms to each study room whereas West had no distinct bedrooms. On the second and third floors there were recitation rooms for the junior and senior classes. The Philologian and Philotechnian literary societies held their meetings, debates, etc., in those rooms but their library remained in West.

On a Sunday afternoon in 1841 while the students were in church, a fire was discovered in the north end of the building. It spread rapidly due to the construction of the building and because there was no readily available water source. An eyewitness account by a member of the class of 1843 states "nearly all that was valuable was saved, except one small library (theological) consisting of about one hundred volumes and the furniture in two or three rooms." Bricks from the old East were used in the next year's construction of the present East and South (now Fayerweather) dormitories, but for inner walls, not fireplaces.

The Hermitage, 1842

Albert Hopkins, professor of astronomy and natural history and brother of President Mark Hopkins, built the first magnetic observatory in 1842. It was a small octagonal building constructed of brick and located near the old site of Hopkins Observatory (therefore close to where Fitch now stands). This observatory was initially used "for ascertaining and exhibiting the laws of Terrestrial Magnetism." When these observations ceased, a student lived there collecting weather statistics. By the 1870s, the Hermitage, as it was then called, was no longer used for scientific purposes and it became a dormitory "occupied by students of a solitary, quiet, and retiring nature who love the wild scenes of the South College ball ground." (*Williams Athenaeum*, May 26, 1883, p. 36). The Hermitage was razed upon the construction of Fitch House (then called Berkshire Hall) in 1905.

Kellogg Hall, 1847

On the low ground, approximately in front of the present Jesup Hall, the small, very plain, sometimes called squat, Kellogg Hall was built. The east-west oriented dormitory was appropriately named since it sat on the site of the college vegetable garden on land purchased and given to the college by Professor Ebenezar Kellogg. The 1847 building was equal in size to one half of East College and initially had two recitation rooms on the first floor for freshmen and sophomores.

This decidedly drab, three-story, box-like structure had no ornamentation or elaborate design, and the accepted practice of college buildings being painted yellow probably only accentuated this fact. President Carter, in his annual report of 1900, stated that Mr. Thompson and Mr. Jesup, whose gifts had created a lab campus, felt that "Kellogg was an obstruction to the view of the laboratories and its general appearance did not harmonize with the style then prevalent." In July of 1900 the building was taken down and its "water faucet" moved to the southeast corner of West College allowing for grading of embankments around Morgan and West and the installation of new sidewalks on the green.

The second gym
See also illustration in main text, p. 45

Cornice and window trim is typical Renaissance Revival

See illustration in main text, p. 67

The Early Gymnasiums, 1851, 1859

Spurred by the development of the new gymnasium movement, and by alumnus David Dudley Field's prodding, Williams' first gymnasium was constructed in 1851 at a cost of $700. The students themselves raised $500 to furnish the equipment: rings, trapeze, ladders, bars, a horse, etc. The students also ran the establishment: "We let them manage it, which they do better than we could," said President Mark Hopkins. A frame structure located on the site of the future Lansing Chapman rink, the building sported a lean-to addition that housed student bathing facilities – actually tin set-tubs with cold running water. The gym burned to the ground in February 1852. Raised on the same spot, a second iteration burned too, in 1858.

Perhaps tired of fires that kept demolishing their facilities, the students next constructed a brick gymnasium. Located at the comer of Spring and Main Streets, it was completed in 1859. Two years later, the College paid off the students' gymnasium debt and assumed ownership of the building. As soon as the first Goodrich Hall was built, however, the brick gym lapsed into use as a service building and, for a number of years, was also used to store the hose used by the student fire brigade. That gym was torn down in 1928 to make way for the addition to Lasell.

Jackson Hall, 1855

On August 14, 1855, members of the Lyceum of Natural History gathered in Jackson Hall to celebrate the 20th anniversary of the student scientific society and the dedication of their new headquarters. The Hall was constructed through funds donated by Nathan Jackson, a generous contributor to a variety of Williams ventures and uncle of James Orton (class of 1855). Orton, a professor of Natural History, eventually lost his life exploring the Amazon.

Located at the southeast corner of the current Berkshire Quadrangle, the main brick building housed the gallery of minerals, shells, skeletons, stuffed birds, etc., gathered by the students, while the tower contained further specimens and the Lyceum's meeting room. Over the door to Jackson Hall was placed a giant bronze eagle, "presented by our generous benefactor, modeled after one exhibited in the United States Crystal Palace, measuring seven feet from tip to tip of the wings and weighting seven hundred pounds." (*Address before the Lyceum of Natural History*, 1855, p. 30). The Hall was torn down in 1908, in part because the college curriculum had absorbed the sciences so well that the Lyceum was fast approaching its demise.

Magnetic Observatory, 1862

The second magnetic observatory, a small rectangular stone tower located near Jackson Hall, was constructed in 1862. "An Electrometer . . . [was] put up near it, for the purpose of determining the amount of electricity in the atmosphere." (*Williams Quarterly*, Nov. 1862, p. 144). The structure lapsed into disuse after 1890 and probably did not last long into the 20th century.

See illustration in main text, p. 49

First Goodrich-4th Gym, 1865

Bowling alleys were available on campus to Williams students during the spring term of 1865. Finished with all the "comforts and conveniences required," the alleys were in a basement room (16 by 96-feet) of the first Goodrich Hall situated on the west side of Griffin. The building, elegant "Early English style," cost approximately $30,000 and on the second floor housed the "best facilities for Gymnastic Exercise and Training" according to the 1866-67 college catalog. In the "Hall" story, within the spacious edifice, there were all the "appliances for gymnastic and military drill" and the room would be used for the Alumni dinner at Commencement.

The entire Chemistry department with classrooms, labs and offices occupied another floor. The building's donor, John Z. Goodrich of Stockbridge, also supplied an additional $25,000 to fund a professorship of Physical Culture. Even though construction of this building proceeded slowly, according to publications of the time, it was done poorly and the building eventually reached the point of being unsafe to use. The Board of Trustees voted in 1902 to take it down and use the old Alumni Hall/Chapel across the Main Street for recitation rooms and religious services.

Thompson Memorial Chapel would be built on the vacated site in 1905. Lasell Gymnasium had been built in 1886 to meet the physical education needs of the students and athletic clubs. The Goodrich name was also transferred to the building across the street in 1905, in appreciation of the donor's continued interest in and generosity to the college.

College Hall, 1872

Constructed in 1872 by H. B. Curtis, College Hall was located on the current site of Stetson Hall and served as a college boarding house until it was razed in 1912. It was a "squat edifice" featuring 22 bedrooms - with priority given to financial aid students - and a Mansard roof in an architectural style that was termed "early North German Lloyd school."

Known as the "hash house," College Hall's infamous reputation for serving the worst food on campus was refuted by F. F. Thompson, class of 1856, when he visited there in 1891: "Mr. Thompson found a seat at the freshman table and was served the same food as the students. The bill of fare consisted of oatmeal with fresh milk from the college farm, beefsteak, well cooked and tender, two kinds of potatoes, four kinds of bread, coffee, etc. The millionaire trustee was well satisfied with his breakfast and thought it compared well with average hotel fare. The cost to the student is $3.25 a week." (*Williams Weekly* 5:165, p. 165)

College Hall was also the scene of various hazing rituals "which rivalled (sic) the Spanish Inquisition for the ingenuity of their barbarity." Some lamented, when the building had outlived its usefulness, that it was not set afire to serve as practice for the student fire brigade.

Field Memorial Observatory, 1882

Perhaps one of the most exotic examples of architecture built for Williams was the second observatory constructed in 1882. This unique example of North Italian Renaissance design and equipment was a memorial gift from David Dudley Field, class of 1825, in honor of his son, an 1850 graduate. The sheet-iron building was placed on a "eminence" southwest of the lab campus on five acres purchased by the college. The location was selected so that there would not be trees on the horizon to obstruct the view through a new Repsold & Son Meridian Circle, which was "fitted with all the very latest improvements."

Sheet iron was selected for the building due to the fact that it was then believed that iron kept an equal temperature for the delicate instruments. Besides the observing room, the building contained two other rooms, which were fitted up for the occupancy of an assistant. Over the years the building fell into disrepair and some of the equipment was removed in 1908, and the rest in 1927 when the site was sold and the building demolished.

Old Clark, 1882

"Thursday night a portion of the outside wall of Clark Hall, on the east side, became loosened by the rain and fell to the ground. Early risers Friday morning were quite surprised to see nearly one-half of the wall from eaves to floor line scattered on the ground." (*North Adams Transcript*, March 21, 1896). Although the college repaired Clark Hall numerous times, the building's poor construction, coupled with the Geology department's desire to share a quad with the other sciences, led to the final destruction of the old Clark Hall in 1907.

Clark Hall had been built on Main Street in 1882 near the site of the present Currier Hall. The building and a cabinet of minerals to be housed there, were paid for by Edward Clark, class of 1831, a Williams trustee and president of the Singer Sewing Machine Company. (Robert Sterling Clark, benefactor of the Clark Art Institute, was Edward's grandson.)

Chadbourne Gymnasium, 1882

Perhaps in an effort to maintain financial resources during a period of national depression, President Paul Chadbourne paid less attention to athletics. As part of his program, he decided to convert (old) Goodrich Hall to classrooms, and build a less impressive wooden frame structure for "physical culture." Thus the Chadbourne gym was erected south of West College and Clark Hall in 1882. The students were not enthusiastic about the gym: "Our gymnasium is undeniably a wretched one, but it is all we are likely to have. . . ." (*Argo*, June 30, 1883, p. 58).

What proves most memorable about this gym are its last days. During Commencement and Reunion activities in 1883 – exercises for both were held during the same period in those years – tables were set up in Chadbourne for the annual alumni dinner. A gale blew up that evening, however, demolishing the gym and smashing crockery, tables and all. Needless to say, student exercise returned to the hall in Goodrich the following year.

Van Rensselaer House, 1894

Ground was broken in March 1894, for a house to accommodate the Sigma Phi fraternity that had lost its previous house to a fire in January 1893. Both houses were located on the site of the present Sawyer Library. The new building was designed by Marcus T. Reynolds, class of 1890, and Charles Rich. The approved plans were for a structure that used materials from the Albany, N.Y., manor house of the Van Rensselaer family.

Reynolds, a descendant of this Dutch patroon family, knew that the deserted mansion was to be destroyed and raised funds to move the salvageable stone and timber to Williamstown. The resulting building resembled the Manor House with adaptations. In 1963, the building was leased to the college for housing that fall and it was officially named the Van Rensselaer House. The Center for Environmental Studies was for a time located in this building that sat on a three-acre site originally purchased from Professor Tatlock, former college librarian. In 1973 Van Rensselaer House was dismantled to accommodate the need for a central campus location for a new library.

(WHT, 1957)

Greylock Hall, 1937

The present Greylock Quad area was at various times the site of a Colonial tavern, a school, and then two successive large hotels that included servants quarters, stables, gardens, etc. These hotels had hosted students, speakers, faculty, and many college functions such as reunions and class dinners. Greylock Hall, an oblong white wooden structure, was the last annex of the hotel that had become college property in 1937. Built in 1916, and adjacent to North Street, it was first used in 1937-38 to house 22 sophomores. All the rooms, except those on the ground floor, had private baths but the college decided not to charge premium room rates at that time.

With the return of the married veterans to campus in 1945 the college converted the dormitory into 12 furnished apartments. Not long after the war it resumed its dorm status. The college closed the structure in anticipation of new construction, but had to reopen it in the fall of 1963 to help alleviate a housing shortage. Knowing that it would eventually be replaced the college did not invest in extensive repairs. Some Greylock Hall residents enhanced their liberal arts education learning how to plaster and paint (supplied by B & G). The "oft-doomed" structure finally was demolished during spring vacation 1964, allowing the five-building residential project on the Greylock corner to proceed. Student residents were offered several housing options for the remainder of the year.

College and Alumni Society Officers

Presidents of Williams

Years of Service	*Name/Class*
1793-1815	Ebenezer Fitch, DD
1815-1821	Zephaniah Swift Moore, DD
1821-1836	Edward Dorr Griffin, DD
1836-1872	Mark Hopkins, 1824, MD, DD, LLD
1872-1881	Paul Ansel Chadbourne, 1848, DD, LLD
1881-1901	Franklin Carter, 1862, PhD, LLD
1901-1902 (actg)	John Haskell Hewitt, 1888, LLD
1902-1908	Henry Hopkins, 1858, DD, LLD
1908-1934	Harry A. Garfield, 1885, LHD, LLD
1934-1937	Tyler Dennett, 1904, PhD, LittD, LLD
1937-1961	James Phinney Baxter 3rd, 1914, PhD, LittD, LHD, DSc, LLD
1961-1973	John E. Sawyer, 1939, MA, LHD, LittD, LLD
1973-1985	John W. Chandler, PhD, LHD, LLD
1985-1993	Francis C. Oakley, PhD, LHD, LittD, LLD
1994-1999	Harry C. Payne, PhD, LittD, LLD
1999-2000	Carl W. Vogt, 1958, LLB, LLD
2000-	Morton Owen Shapiro, MA, PhD, LHD, LLD

Secretaries
The Society of Alumni

Years of Service	*Name/Class*
1821-1826	Charles A. Dewey, 1811
1826-1828	Charles Baker, 1820
1828-1838	Henry L. Sabin, 1821 (Pro Tem)
1838-1852	Edward Lasell, 1828
1852-1877	Nathaniel Herrick Griffin, 1834
1877-1879	John Lemeuel Thomas Phillips, 1847
1879-1890	Arthur L. Perry, 1852
1890-1909	Eben B. Parsons, 1859 (Pro Tem)
1909-1919	William C. Hart, 1894
1919-1935	E. Herbert Botsford, 1882
1935-1947	Edwin H. Adriance, 1914
1947-1950	Alfred L. Jarvis, 1939
1950-1951	Whitney S. Stoddard, 1935
1951-1961	Charles B. Hall, 1915
1961-1975	John P. English, 1932
1975-1986	R. Cragin Lewis, 1941
1986-1992	Robert V. Behr, 1955
1992-1998	Chester K. Lasell, 1958
1998-	Wendy W. Hopkins, 1972

Presidents
Society of Alumni

Monuments

The Haystack Monument in Mission Park

The American Missionary Society's 150th anniversary observance (WHT, 1956)

Soldiers' Monument on original base (WCA, c. 1883)

The Soldier today

The Haystack Monument, 1867

The late 18th and early 19th century saw an increase in religious fervor on college campuses. This movement started in Connecticut and spread to the rest of the country. At Williams this enthusiasm took the form of student prayer meetings held twice weekly in Sloan's Meadow on the north edge of the campus. At one of these meetings, in August of 1806, five students (Samuel J. Mills, James Richards, Francis L. Robbins, Harvey Loomis and Byram Green) took refuge from a sudden thunderstorm in the lee of a large haystack. Their classroom studies of Asia and the East India Company had led them to conclude that Christianity should be sent abroad and they prayed that American missions would take up this task. Their haystack discussion led to the creation of the American missionary movement.

To commemorate this dramatic event a 12-foot tall marble monument, topped by a globe signifying the universal involvement of their efforts, was dedicated by President Mark Hopkins following Baccalaureate in 1867. The base carries the inscription "The Field is the World," a depiction of a haystack and the statement "The Birthplace of American Foreign Missions 1806." The monument sits in a pine grove at the approximate location of Sloan's Meadow in a section of the campus known as Mission Park.

The Soldiers' Monument, 1868

Williams College was the first educational institution in the country to honor those who lost their lives in the Civil War. The Soldiers' Monument in front of Griffin Hall was dedicated in 1868 after the Society of Alumni had raised the nearly $10,000 to pay for it. It was modelled by James G. Batterson of Hartford and cast at the Ames foundry in Chicopee. A photograph shows the monument standing on an octagonal sandstone base with a series of buttresses acting as a pedestal for the eight-foot bronze statue. The height of pedestal and statue was an imposing 25 feet.

In the early 1920s, when Main Street was lowered to reduce the elevation of Consumption Hill, the monument had to be moved. The sandstone pedestal was eroded and couldn't be moved. The base was taken apart and the pieces were thrown off the Walley Bridge into the Green River. The statue was stored until 1926 when the Trustees donated the money to have Cram and Ferguson design a new base and the monument was re-erected with the soldier turned slightly to face directly south. In 1928, the monument was rededicated with a block dance for the town held on Spring Street.

Civil War monuments are difficult to create because of the complexity of the Union uniforms. This sculptor seems to have held this statue together through the placement of the musket, the twist of the torso and the use of a generic Union cap. There is even a wonderful swirl to his mustache.

The Gargoyle Gate at Weston Field

The Hopkins Gate (NW)

The Symmes Gate (TWB)

The Gargoyle Gate, 1906

The Gargoyle Society, which was founded in 1896, had as its main goal: "to serve the College in any way that would further its mission." The entrance to Weston Field had been an uncontrolled opening, with no way to sell or collect tickets or to manage the flow of pedestrian or carriage traffic in and out. The Gargoyle members recognized this problem and raised the money to build the gate as a solution.

The architects were Frederick A. Squires, class of 1900, and John Wynkoop. Squires later became a geologist, and clearly had an appreciation for William's picturesque environs, designing "a sturdy building to hold its own where the natural surroundings were on so great a scale."

The gate was designed to separate foot and carriage traffic, with the help of local policemen on the street outside the field. Constructed at the west entrance to Weston Field in 1905 and 1906, the gate is purported to have been designed based on French Gothic architecture. It consists of a round section with ticket windows that served both foot and vehicular traffic lines. Carriages went past on the open east side and pedestrians went under a low central arch. A small security office was located in a square pier which supported the west end of the arch.

The Hopkins Gate, 1927

This memorial to the brothers Mark and Albert Hopkins was the 1927 gift of Albert's daughter Susan, and is located below the east facade of West College on what is known as Lab Campus Drive. Its inscription reads: "Climb High, Climb Far, Your Goal the Sky, Your Aim the Star." These words were found by Susan as she was going through her late father's papers, but there is nothing to indicate that either of the Hopkins brothers wrote them. In fact, their origin remains unknown.

The gate itself consists of two granite piers, capped by urns, at the bottom of a series of steps. At the top is a metal arch surmounted by a replication of a lantern.

The gate was created by a stonemason family from Gloucester: designed by Caroll Coletti, built by his brother Paul, with the inscriptions believed to have been cut by another brother, Joseph. At the conclusion of Commencement exercises the graduating seniors walk between facing lines of faculty at the top of the steps and then pass through the gate in their first act as alumni.

The Symmes Gate, 1936

On January 24, 1935, in below zero weather off the coast of New Jersey, a tragedy occurred which involved Williams students and faculty. The *Mohawk*, a steamship of Panamanian registration, collided with a freighter and sank almost immediately, taking with it three undergraduates and Geology Professor Herdman Cleland. The students who died, all seniors, were William B. Symmes, Julius Palmer and Lloyd H. Crowfoot. Four other students, members of what was to be a geologic expedition to the Mayan ruins in the Yucatan, survived. Incidently, all seven were to take their mid-year exams in all courses while they were en route, under the supervision of Professor Cleland.

A year later, on January 25, 1936, a beautiful gate was dedicated. It was given as a memorial to the accident victims by Mr. and Mrs. William Dwight Symmes Jr. of New York City, the parents of Bill Symmes.

This gate, brick piers supporting hand wrought-iron panels, connects the western wings of Williams and Sage Halls, closing off that side of the freshman quadrangle. The central section contains large iron gates which open and close under a wrought iron arch which is especially detailed and fascinating. On each side, brick and ironwork walls connect the gate with the buildings.

Former Fraternity Properties

Graduate Art Student Dormitory (Phi Sigma Kappa)

Thirteen houses which were once the homes of fraternities are now owned by Williams, and in one case Williamstown, and they serve the College and the community in ways as varied as their origins and their architectural styles.

The Phi Sigma Kappa fraternity built this simple brick Tudor style building on South Street adjacent to the Clark Art Institute in 1931. It is now known as Fort Hoosac and housed Williams undergraduates from 1963 until 1982. Since then it has housed some of the first-year students in the Graduate Program in the History of Art

The program's College website states that Williams, in cooperation with the Sterling and Francine Clark Art Institute, offers a two-year course of study leading to the degree of Master of Arts in the history of art. The objective of the program, started in 1972, is to prepare students for academic and museum careers, and equip them for further study and research, independently or at other institutions.

Students must complete a minimum of 11 courses and two winter study periods (a European study trip in the first year and a qualifying paper in the second). Every student must also achieve reading proficiency in German and one other foreign language.

Through a work/study program, students may work in a curatorial department, as a teaching or research assistant, or in the Williamstown Art Conservation Center. Study-related employment is available through assistantships at the Clark, the Williams College Museum of Art, the

Chapin Rare Book Library, and MASS MoCA (Massachusetts Museum of Contemporary Art), and through teaching assistantships in undergraduate survey courses.

Recent graduates have pursued doctorates at Columbia, Harvard, MIT, NYU, Stanford, Berkeley, University of Chicago, University of Pennsylvania and Yale, or taken jobs at such institutions as the Getty Museum, the Philadelphia Museum of Art, the Walker Art Center, the Albright-Knox Art Gallery, the Art Institute of Chicago, the Clark, the Corcoran Gallery of Art and the Metropolitan Museum of Art.

Agard House
(Delta Phi)

Delta Phi, located on South Street, was built in the 1920s in a sort of Queen Anne style. Now known as Agard it is a College dormitory. It has a medieval character with a stair tower and overhanging roofs. Ample porches surround the living room.

Center for Development
Economics (Delta Psi)

Delta Psi, later known at St. Anthony Hall and The Saint House, was designed by Stanford White of the firm of McKim, Mead & White. Off the southeast corner of Field Park, the building is now the home of the Center for Development Economics. Constructed in 1885, the building was expanded in 1906 when a wing was added to the south side. White's work here is the final iteration of a style which had absorbed his efforts since his early decorative collaboration with H. H. Richardson a decade before on the Watts Sherman house (1874) in Newport. This is one of the most distinguished buildings on the Williams campus.

Henry J. Bruton, John J. Gibson Professor of Economics, emeritus, and former director of the CDE, describes the program:

"One of the truly great questions of the day is this: Why are some few countries in the world enormously rich and others so abysmally poor? This question has implications for all aspects of contemporary existence, peace and war, political stability, health and welfare, and basic morality. The CDE is concerned with seeking to understand this basic question and then how a poor people may go about so modifying their economy that a more humane and rewarding economic performance is achieved.

"The basic idea of the Center for Development Economics is both simple and subtle: gather a group of 25 or so up-and-

coming young civil servants from Asia, Africa, Latin America, and Eastern Europe in an educational community devoted to liberal arts teaching and learning, provide a first rate, devoted faculty with demanding, carefully crafted reading and writing assignments, and constant discussion, debate, probing, and worrying. After nine months of this sort of intensive activity, a more mature, informed, capable civil servant emerges. The year here we do believe turns out a person who is much better able to appreciate his/her country's problems and identify ways and means to go about overcoming them than they were on their arrival.

"The CDE House, once Saint Anthony's, is an ideal place for this sort of program. Its beautiful living room and splendid dining room provide ample public space for relaxation and talk and fun. The class room upstairs is an excellent ambient for lecture, discussion, and all the routines of searching and learning. There is also ample space for computers, so essential for modern study. Finally the more than 20 bedrooms provide comfortable living arrangements for participants and facilitate the never ending discussion that learning entails.

"Some time ago a Williams alumnus of the 1950s who was a member of Saint Anthony's visited the CDE and later remarked that the building now was more saintly than ever before. It is easy to agree with that statement."

Garfield House (Delta Upsilon)

This South Street home was purchased by Delta Upsilon in 1924 and remodled to house the fraternity. It is now a College dormitory named Garfield House and has recently had an elevator added to its north side to make it handicapped accessible. It simulates late English gothic beam and stucco construction and has a stair tower and multiple porches, with an emphasis on vertical lines.

Williamstown Town Hall
(Phi Gamma Delta)

Now the Williamstown Town Hall, the former home of Phi Gamma Delta is located just north of Field Park. The fraternity built the house in 1928 and sold it to the town in 1965 to house the offices of local government. The basic rectangular shape of the building has flanking wings on either side of a central section containing the main entrance. It gives the impression of Georgian campus revival.

Perry House
(Alpha Delta Phi)

Built in 1896 by Alpha Delta Phi, this is on the site of the original Victorian Gothic fraternity designed in 1869 by Russell Sturgis. The original was incorporated in the present structure. Large additions were put on in 1905 and in 1913. The architect for the first was Jerome K. Allen, class of 1895. This yellow brick structure is now a College dormitory called Perry House.

Weston Language Center
(Phi Delta Theta)

Phi Delta Theta built this home in 1907 from a purportedly prize-winning design by the New York firm of Squires & Wynkoop, architects of the Gargoyle Gate. It is certainly the tallest of the former fraternity houses with three full stories and a large attic. The building has lots of classical details, especially on the porch, and decorative Rockwood Pottery tiling around some of the windows. A new dining hall was added to the south side in the 1920s. Now the Weston Language Center, it is named after Karl E. Weston, class of 1896, who taught French for several years before becoming head of the College's Art Department. The cellar contains modern langauge labs and the old dining room serves as a large meeting/teaching room. Other rooms are used as language faculty offices and classrooms.

Wood House
(Zeta Psi)

Built by Zeta Psi in 1907, this building on the corner of South and Main Streets was designed by William Neil Smith and is now called Wood House. A dormitory, the house is dominated by a two-story, pedimented portico with classical orders. The Corinthian capitals wore out and were replaced by simpler capitals because there was no carver available on the College staff. The facade could be called "academic Georgian."

Bascom House
(Beta Theta Pi)

This Colonial/Georgian home for the Beta Theta Pi fraternity was built in 1913. Designed by Harding and Seaver, it is now a dormitory known as Bascom House. The two-story brick structure has elaborate dormers and a detailed doorway and large porch on the south side. It is on the west side of Stetson Court.

(TWB)

(ABG)

(ABG)

Brooks House
(Delta Kappa Epsilon)

Following a spectacular fire in January of 1959, which destroyed the Delta Kappa Epsilon house with its monumental pedimented facade, a new home for the fraternity was built and occupied in 1961. The present facade appears to have been designed by an architect who might have had a Mt. Vernon complex. Now a dormitory, Brooks House is a two-story building which has a basement that opens onto ground level in the rear and houses the administrative offices of a very busy Summer Conference program.

Spencer House
(Chi Psi)

In 1908 a new Chi Psi house was built on the corner of Hoxsey and Main and the former fraternity home, just across Hoxsey Street, became the faculty club. The new house was designed by architect James Purdon. With a concrete frame and brick facing it became the first fireproof fraternity building on campus. The exterior is predominantly Georgian, with ornamented pediments, elaborate quoining on the corners, and classical porches and doorways. It is now a dormitory named Spencer House.

Mears House
(Theta Delta Chi)

In 1926 Theta Delta Chi built a simplified Georgian style house on Park Street, designed by Cram and Ferguson. Obviously it is meant to fit in with the nearby Sage and Williams Halls which that firm had also designed. It does this admirably. The building, Mears House, now contains the offices of the Society of Alumni and the College's development officers. Two former out-buildings on the west side have been converted to provide additional office space.

Tyler House
(Psi Upsilon)

Now called Tyler House, this building (see Tyler, 1972, in main text) was designed by architects Andrews, Jones, Biscoe and Whitmore of Boston in 1927 to serve as the home of Psi Upsilon. Reminiscent of the Tudor style, the house has steep, unornamented gables and, with its addition, serves today as a major dormitory unit.

Williams
Outside
the
Berkshires

(Mystic Press Photos)

Numbers 2 and 4 Lathbury Road house a faculty apartment, student rooms and a library (Reichert Photos)

The Williams-Mystic Program in American Maritime Studies

The Williams-Mystic Program in American Maritime Studies opened in September 1977 with 21 students from Williams, Smith, Mt. Holyoke, Middlebury and nine other small liberal arts colleges in New England. The program's founding director was Williams History Professor Benjamin W. Labaree, who wanted undergraduates to have an opportunity to focus a semester of their college program on the sea.

While living in cooperative houses at Mystic Seaport, the nation's leading maritime museum, they take Williams College courses in maritime history, literature of the sea, marine science, and marine policy. In addition, they spend 10 days offshore on board a research schooner, a week exploring the California (fall semester) or Oregon and Washington (spring semester) coasts, and a long weekend at a research facility on Nantucket.

The museum is located on the Connecticut coast, close to a wide range of marine habitats and has a first-rate library and marine sciences laboratory.

The present director is Williams Professor of Marine Sciences James T. Carlton, who has a world-wide reputation in the field of biological invasions.

The Williams-Oxford Program

Judy Reichert, wife of former director of The Williams-Oxford Program, describes the program:

"The Williams-Oxford Program gives two dozen Williams students an opportunity to experience the Oxford tutorial system, in which one or two students meet weekly with an Oxford don to present an essay which forms the basis of a critical discussion. Each student usually enrolls in five tutorials during the year, frequently in subjects of his or her own design. (So popular has this method of teaching proven to be that most departments at Williams now offer at least one tutorial each year.)

"Students are affiliated with Exeter College, Oxford, which enables them to participate in the social, cultural and athletic life of the university. Ephraim Williams House, where the students live, is located about one and a half miles north of the center of Oxford – an easy bicycle ride. Built around a courtyard, the complex includes residences, a library, computer room, common room and dining facilities, as well as the Director's House. Two or more Exeter students usually live in a Williams residence, facilitating interaction between Williams and Exeter students.

"Two six-week vacation periods between Michaelmas, Hilary and Trinity terms give students a chance to travel in Britain and on the continent, or simply to enjoy the glories of Oxford, the nearby Cotswolds, and London.

Number 1 Moreton Road is the John Reichert House, the home of the Williams-Oxford directors

The entrance on West 39th Street (Williams Club Photo)

Promotional brochure for the relocated club (WCA, c. 1924)

The Williams Club of New York

"The Director, a Williams faculty member, serves for two years. My husband held the position from 1993 to 1995. The day after we arrived, exhausted, the Program's solicitor (lawyer) escorted us to the boat races at Henley. He kindly supplied a hat for me, as a clueless American, and warned me that no trousers and no skirts above the knee were acceptable at Henley.

"That was the beginning of a two-year learning experience which included mastering the creation of summer pudding and marmalade, driving on the left, and distinguishing Norman from Gothic architecture, but never extended to the love of Marmite.

"The students neither wanted nor needed 'mothering' but they enjoyed an occasional dinner at the Director's House. We saw plays, operas and historic sights together. Best of all, though, was our annual hike from Bibury to Coin St. Aldwyn, pub lunch included.

"Not many students set their alarms to awaken early for May Morning, but those who do arrive at Magdalen Bridge at 6 a.m., when an angelic choir welcomes May from the tower, little girls wander about in flower-trimmed hats, and Morris dancers perform in the streets for crowds of Oxford students in fancy dress from the balls of the previous night. It is quintessential, magical England."

Editor's note: The Williams-Oxford Program started in 1985 after the College purchased the property of a defunct tutoring school.

Walk south on Park Avenue from Grand Central, up past the Whitney Museum's gallery on the right, the automobile ramp on the left, the office towers of the lower Avenue on both sides, then turn the corner into 39th Street. Now head west. There, two-thirds of the way down the block on the left, at Number 24, you will see a purple flag waving over the entrance to the Williams Club of New York.

The club was originally around the corner at 291 Madison in an Edith Wharton era brownstone. James Phinney Baxter 3rd '14, represented the students at the opening ceremonies for the Madison Avenue building on Dec. 12, 1913.

A dozen years later the Club moved into two adjoining six-story, 19th-century brownstones on 39th Street. The entrance was three steps down from street level. Inside to the left was the front desk. To the right was – and still is – a dark-paneled room beneath whose floorboards, hoary rumor has it, liquor was stashed during Prohibition. Beneath those same boards and others throughout the building lived occasional dinner fare for the house cat.

In the late 1980s a major renovation removed the need for the cat and provided members with a truly gracious venue. The entrance now caps a 10-step staircase from the street and opens into an elegant high-ceilinged hallway, a spacious reception lounge and library. In the rear are the elevator, cloakroom and dining rooms. On the second floor there are five conference rooms. On the next three floors are 28 bedrooms, including two suites. On the sixth floor is the Club's largest open space – a room capable of holding more than 100 – with city views to both north and south.

The economics of operating a hostelry or restaurant in Manhattan are always exacting. During the Depression, College President Garfield wrote the membership to thank them for the scholarship aid they had provided "in these lean years." And the editor of the Club's newsletter spoke sorrowfully "of taking in another college as a blood transfusion." So the Club experimented with extending its facilities to groups from other colleges, including Amherst. In 1939 MIT's Tech club was welcomed on a rental basis. In 1943, women began being admitted.

In 1961, the Dartmouth Club visited for six months while its own new quarters were being readied. And in 1962, the Hamilton Club was accepted as an affiliate.

By the year 2000 the number of affiliated clubs had grown to 50, but Williams men and women still accounted for more than 60 percent of the 4,000 members. And the Club's board continued to be 100 percent purple.

Submitted by R. Rhett Austell Jr. '48, former president of the Williams Club.

Building to
Enrollment Graph

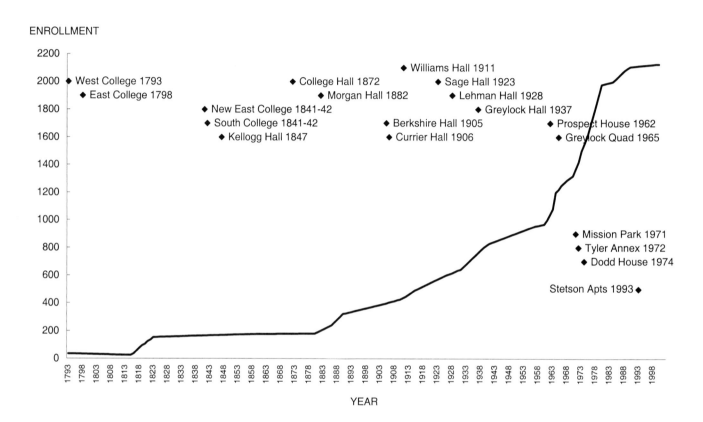

ENROLLMENT

Note: Enrollment figures are approximations based on available data.

Selected Bibliography

Adriance, Vanderpoel. *New Foundations*. Williamstown, Mass.: [s.n.], 1940.

Benjamin, Asher. *A Reprint of "The Builder's Assistant,"* "*The American Builder's Companion,*" "*The Rudiments of Architecture,*" "*The Practical House Carpenter,*" "*Practice of Architecture.*" New York: The Architectural Book Publishing Co., P. Wenzel and M. Krakow, 1917.

Brooks, Robert R.R., ed. *Williamstown, the First Two Hundred Years, 1753–1953, and Twenty Years Later, 1953–1973*. 2d ed. Williamstown, Mass.: Williamstown Historical Commission, 1974.

Friedman, Terry. *James Gibbs*. New Haven, Conn.: Published for Paul Mellon Centre for Studies in British Art by Yale Univ. Press, 1984.

Harman, Mac. "Stone Chapel/Goodrich Hall Timeline/Facilities History." Student paper, Williams College, 1998. Also available [Online]: <http://www.williams.edu/library/archives/buildinghistories/goodrich/history.html> [2000].

Holden, Reuben Andrus. *Yale: A Pictorial History*. New Haven, Conn.: Yale Univ. Press, 1967.

Johnson, Eugene J., ed. *Charles Moore: Buildings and Projects, 1949–1986*. New York: Rizzoli, 1986.

Lewis, R. Cragin, ed. *Williams, 1793–1993: A Pictorial History*. Williamstown, Mass.: Williams College Bicentennial Commission, 1993.

Malmstrom, R.E. *Lawrence Hall at Williams College*. Williamstown, Mass.: Williams College Museum of Art, [1979].

Mayhew, Ryan. "Jesup Hall." Student paper, Williams College, 2000. Also available [Online]: <http://www.williams.edu/library/archives/buildinghistories/jesup/index.html> [2000].

McElvein, Bruce Burr. "Williams College Architecture, 1790-1860." 2 vols. B.A. thesis, Williams College, 1979.

Perry, Arthur Latham. *Williamstown and Williams College*. 3d ed. Norwood, Mass.: Norwood Press, 1904.

Pierson, William Harvey. *American Buildings and their Architects*. 4 vols. Garden City, N.Y.: Doubleday, 1970–1978.

Rudolph, Frederick. *Mark Hopkins and the Log: Williams College, 1836–1872*. Bicentennial edition. Williamstown, Mass.: Williams College, 1996.

Rudolph, Frederick, ed. *Perspectives: A Williams Anthology*. Williamstown, Mass.: Williams College, 1983.

Sizer, Theodore. *The Works of Colonel John Trumbull*, Artist of the American Revolution. New Haven, Conn.: Yale Univ. Press, 1951.

Warren, Philip H., Jr. *What's In a Name: The Buildings of Williams College: A Collection of Essays*. Williamstown, Mass.: Williams College, 1999.

Warren, Philip H., Jr., comp. "Williams College: Bicentennial Bench Marks." *Williams Alumni Review*, v. 85, no. 2 (Winter 1993): Supplement.

Index

Page numbers in *italic* refer to illustrations.